Learn Hebrew

for Adult Beginners

Speak Hebrew in 30 Days!

3 Books in 1

Explore to Win

THIS COLLECTION INCLUDES

THE FOLLOWING BOOKS:

Complete Hebrew Workbook for Adult Beginners:
Read Hebrew in 30 Days!

Complete Hebrew Workbook for Adult Beginners:
Write Hebrew in 30 Days!

Complete Hebrew Workbook for Adult Beginners:
Speak Hebrew in 30 Days!

Table of Contents

BOOK 1

Complete Hebrew Workbook for Adult Beginners: Reading

BOOK 2

Complete Hebrew Workbook for Adult Beginners: Writing

BOOK 3

Complete Hebrew Workbook for Adult Beginners: Speaking

$100+ FREE BONUSES

100 Hebrew Flash Cards

100 Hebrew Audio Pronunciations

Hebrew 30-Day Study Plan

Hebrew Conversations Narrated

Scan QR code to claim your bonuses

— OR —

visit bit.ly/4c45dQG

BOOK 1

Complete Hebrew Workbook for Adult Beginners: **Reading**

Read Hebrew in 30 Days!

Explore to Win

Introduction

מָבוֹא

(MaVo)

A new language is a new life.

שָׂפָה חֲדָשָׁה הִיא חַיִּים חֲדָשִׁים

You hold this book because learning Hebrew intrigues you, and rightly so. It's one of the most ancient languages still spoken, much like Latin or ancient Greek. Yet today, not only is it a linguistic relic, but also the vibrant language of a thriving Middle Eastern country and top tourist destination. Hebrew shares roots with languages like Arabic. It has been shaped by, and has shaped, historical conversations for millennia. Despite being spoken by only around 10 million people globally, Hebrew is a central cultural pillar in modern Western society.

Yet Hebrew stands apart from any other Western language. It carries a unique alphabet that's neither a variant of the Roman characters seen in Romance (Spanish, Italian, French) and Germanic languages (English, Dutch, Swedish, etc.) nor a derivative of the Cyrillic system used in many Slavic languages (such as Russian or Ukrainian). Hebrew's structure, syntax, and phonetics are also distinct. Reading from right to left, unfamiliar sounds and sentence structures, writing without vowels – all these are foreign to the modern Western reader.

The idea of mastering a new alphabet and a unique reading and speaking system can seem overwhelming or intimidating. It may seem like a daunting challenge left only for esoteric academics and die-hard polyglots. *But* – with this book, you can prove the exact opposite. Learning Hebrew can be effortless, enjoyable, and even fun. How? The methodology of this book will be broken down into easily managed, bite-sized sections. We will progress step-by-step, beginning with the basics.

Starting with the basics, you will be able to unlock the ancient yet vibrant language of Hebrew in just 30 days with this learning series: *Learn Hebrew for Adult Beginners: 3 Books in 1*. This series is meticulously crafted to transform absolute beginners into confident speakers and readers. And it was written by a native speaker who "gets" how difficult it is to learn Hebrew as a second language.

This series is not just about memorizing words and rules; it's about immersing yourself in the Hebrew language and culture. Whether your goal is to connect with your heritage, prepare for travel, or simply learn a new and exciting language, these books will guide you every step of the way.

A Brief History: Ancient and Modern

Hebrew, with its storied past, is more than just a language; it's a journey through history, and that's not just a cliché. Originating as a Semitic language closely related to Phoenician and Moabite, Hebrew was the spoken and written language of the ancient Hebrew people, who later became known as Israelites and, subsequently, Jews. This language has a rich heritage, dating back to the second millennium BCE.

Initially, Hebrew was dynamically used both in speech and writing. It was employed for sacred texts, like the Bible, and was the vernacular until around the destruction of the First Temple in 587 BCE. Afterwards, its role transitioned primarily to a literary and liturgical language.

One fascinating aspect of Hebrew is its script. The language experienced a shift from an earlier script, referred to as *ktav ivri* (כתב עברי), to what is known as ktav ashuri (כתב אשורי), the Assyrian script, which is the block letter form familiar in Torah scrolls and most printed texts today. Despite these changes in script, the fundamental spelling and grammatical system of Hebrew remained relatively consistent. The pronunciation, too, likely stayed similar over the centuries, although the exact sounds of ancient Hebrew are a subject of scholarly debate.

The latter script, "ktav ashuri," will be what we will be studying in this series.

Throughout its history, Hebrew absorbed influences from other languages, like Greek, Latin, and Persian, especially during the Mishnaic and Medieval periods. These influences were evident in some changes in grammar and the addition of new vocabulary. Yet for the last 25000 years, Hebrew remained mostly just a written language, used in religious texts, correspondence, and prayers, and was seldom spoken. Jewish communities adapted to the local languages and cultures, sometimes integrating, sometimes remaining separate, and at times facing persecution.

The revival of Hebrew as a spoken language is a remarkable story. In the late 19th century, as Zionism gained momentum and the idea of a Jewish state began to take shape, Eliezer Ben-Yehuda, a European Jew, began to push for the resurrection of Hebrew. Many were skeptical, some even suggesting German as Israel's official language, but Ben-Yehuda persisted. He published the first modern Hebrew dictionary in 1908, a monumental effort that continued beyond his death, culminating in 17 volumes by 1958. The Academy of the Hebrew Language, established thereafter, continues to oversee the development of Hebrew, ensuring its grammatical integrity and modern vocabulary relevance.

Thanks to Ben-Yehuda's efforts and the cultural revolution of the early 20th century Zionist movement, Hebrew is not just a relic of the past but a living, modern language. When you study this book, you will literally be speaking in the language of people that existed thousands of years ago.

A Matter of Structure

I intimately understand how learning Hebrew from scratch can feel like an uphill journey. When I was 15, I started learning Hebrew, and it seemed daunting at first, especially the speaking part. The switch in mindset that Hebrew required was initially a hurdle, but once I embraced it, the language opened up to me in an unexpectedly straightforward way. This was a revelation during my years in Israel, both as a student and later as a teacher of Hebrew for newcomers to the culture.

But what was the secret? For me, it was the *systematic* nature of the language.

Think of it as a beautifully intricate puzzle where each piece fits perfectly. Eliezer Ben-Yehuda's work, along with the Academy of Hebrew, has made this puzzle easier to solve. They have ensured that Hebrew remained rule-based, with only a number of minor exceptions, making it simpler than you might initially think. *Especially* when you compare it to the complexities of modern English, for example.

Yes, the rules are *different* than English. I would argue, however, that English is a *much* more difficult language to learn than Hebrew is. The rules in English are both far greater in number, and less binding in actuality. Hebrew is all about simplicity and structure. There are basic spelling rules that do not change. There are some basic grammar rules and sentence structure rules; the exceptions are few and easy to remember.

My personal journey has not only led me to a career in translation but has also fueled my desire to share this knowledge. In this book, I aim to convey not just the technical aspects of Hebrew but also the joy and satisfaction that come from unlocking its secrets. As you turn these pages and begin, remember that this is not just about learning a language; it's about connecting with a piece of living history and making it your own.

This Book: The Alphabet (or, the *Alef-Bet*)

It's important to note that the Hebrew alphabet is called the *Alef-Bet* (בית-אלף) *and* has remained consistent for at least 2000 years. This consistency is evident from the Masoretic TaNaKh, the Hebrew Bible (or Hebrew *Old Testament*), which has been replicated for over two millennia using the same Alef-Bet, the same system, the same spelling rules, the same syntax, and some of the original vocabulary. To fully grasp Hebrew – at all – we must start with the Alef-Bet.

You might find the Hebrew alphabet (Alef-Bet) more familiar than expected. Similar to how the word "alphabet" originates from the first two Greek letters (*alpha* and *beta*), the term "Alef-Bet" comes from the first two Hebrew letters, **alef** (א) and **bet** (ב). The Hebrew Alef-Bet comprises 22 basic letters in its simplest form. As seven of the letters have one or two variations, the total number of letters we will learn is 31. The first 22 are (from right to left):

Alef	Bet	Gimel	Dalet	He	Vav	Zayin	Chet	Tet	Yod	Kaf
א	ב	ג	ד	ה	ו	ז	ח	ט	י	כ ך

Lamed	Mem	Nun	Samech	Ayin	Pe	Tsadi	Qof	Resh	Shin	Tav
ל	מ	נ	ס	ע	פ	צ	ק	ר	ש	ת

Tav	Shin	Resh	Qof	Tsadi	Pe	Ayin	Samekh	Nun	Mem	Lamed

The variations of the letters ב, כ, מ, נ, פ, צ, ש add nine more symbols to the alphabet:

ש	צ	פ	פ	נ	מ	כ	כ	ב
Shin	Tsade	Fe	Fe	Nun	Mem	Khaf	Khaf	Vet
שׂ	ץ	ף	פ֧	ן	ם	ך	כּ	בּ
Sin	Tsade Sofit	Fe Sofit	Pe	Nun Sofit	Mem Sofit	Khaf Sofit	Kaf	Bet

In addition to these consonants, Hebrew also has a vowel system comprising 14 symbols (for our purposes), which represent five basic sounds. These vowels are crucial for proper pronunciation and understanding:

(Stop)													
אְ	אוּ	אֻ	אוֹ	אֹ	אִי	אִ	אֱ	אֵ	אֶ	אֲ	אָ	אַ	אָ
---	OO		OH		EE		EH			AH			

And that's it. Everything in this first book revolves around the letters and vowels you see on this page. By mastering them, you'll be well on your way to reading, writing, and speaking in Hebrew fluently. With time and practice, they will become more approachable (and less intimidating!).

~

This book is your comprehensive guide. Mastering the Alef-Bet.

- In this book, each chapter will introduce a set of Hebrew letters and vowels.

- After each chapter, you'll learn basic words and be able to practice the main concepts covered.

- The chapters are designed to build upon each other, so it is important to follow them in sequential order.

- By the end of this book, you will not only know the Alef-Bet, but also many words and grammatical rules.

The upcoming chapter is the bedrock for the rest of the book – your key that you can return to as needed. It's designed to make the learning process both structured and engaging, and ensure a solid grasp of the basics. Whether you are a complete beginner or have some prior knowledge, this book aims to enrich your proficiency and comprehension. Let's get started.

~

Embrace the challenge today.

Experience the joy of speaking Hebrew in just 30 days.

Chapter 1 – Rules for Reading

If you grab too much, you grab nothing.

תָּפַשְׂתָּ לֹא תָּפַשְׂתָּ מְרֻבֶּה

First Things First: Three Concepts

In the following chapter, we will lay the groundwork for your Hebrew learning journey. To ensure a smooth start, there are three fundamental concepts you need to familiarize yourself with. **First**, Hebrew uses a system of dots and dashes known as **'Nikud'** to indicate vowels. These marks appear beneath, within, or above the consonants. We'll introduce these vowel markers gradually and help you to integrate them naturally into your reading. **Second**, unlike English, Hebrew is read and written **from right to left**. This might feel counterintuitive at first, but with practice, it will become second nature. Pay special attention to the direction of the text in the examples and exercises throughout this book. Third, transliteration. This involves representing Hebrew sounds using our Latin alphabet. Further on, you will find transliteration rules for the Hebrew words in this series to aid your understanding of their pronunciation. Familiarize yourself with how each Hebrew letter and vowel point is represented in English. Remember, transliterations are only a guide; the goal is to become comfortable reading the Hebrew script directly!

Hidden Vowels (Nikud)

Originally, Hebrew was written without vowels, a characteristic of many Semitic languages. The script, primarily consonantal, demanded a thorough understanding of context and language structure for correct pronunciation. For example, in ancient Hebrew, the word *shalom* (שלום), which means "hello," "goodbye," or "peace," would have been written as:

" SH L M "

The only issue was that this required highly contextualized reading skills. This is because "SH-L-M" could also refer to *shalem* (שלם), which means "complete" or "pay." It could even refer to *shulam*

(שולם), which means "paid." As Hebrew evolved, particularly with the intent to preserve religious texts and ensure accurate reading and pronunciation, the system of *Nikud* was introduced. If *Nikud* were to be used on our English *shalom* example, it would look like this:

$$\overset{\text{O}}{\text{``SHLM''}}\underset{\text{A}}{}$$

Here, the "A" under the "SH" (Shin – שׁ) represents the 'ah' sound, and the "O" above the "L" (Lamed - ל) signifies the 'oh' sound, making it easier to pronounce. Here are some other examples:

5. Shabbat (שבת), or "sabbath" in English, is the Jewish day of rest – on Saturday:

$$\underset{\text{A \ A}}{\text{``SH B T''}}$$

6. *Kasher* (כשר), or "kosher" in English, is the system of Jewish dietary laws that include laws against eating pigs.

$$\underset{\text{A \ \ E}}{\text{``K SH R''}}$$

7. Hallelujah (הללויה) is a word signifying praise and glory toward God in the Hebrew Bible, in the book of Psalms:

$$\underset{\text{A E U A}}{\text{``H L L Y''}}$$

8. Modern Hebrew has incorporated common modern words such as "internet" (אינטרנט) and "telephone" (טלפון), among many others:

$$\underset{\text{I \ \ \ E \ \ \ E}}{\text{``N T R N T''}}$$

&

$$\overset{\text{O}}{\text{``T L F N''}}\underset{\text{E \ E}}{}$$

The Hebrew Nikud is a series of dots and dashes that are added to the consonants to indicate vowel sounds.[1] This feature will come to our advantage in the learning process, since Hebrew is refreshingly straightforward when it comes to spelling. Unlike English, which often has complex and seemingly illogical spellings, Hebrew is much more phonetic and consistent. If we were to apply the Hebrew spelling approach to the English word "apple," for example, it would be more like "apel" or even "apl" with the vowels indicated by Nikud. The word "night" is another good example. If it were spelled in the Hebrew method, it would probably be "nait" (or even NT with nikd signifying the "ay" and "ee" sounds). There's no silent 'gh' or any other non-phonetic complexities. A good English example that follows the Hebrew method is "river," which is spelled more or less how it sounds: "riv-er."

It's also helpful to understand that Nikud is mostly used in educational materials, religious texts, and literature for children or language learners. In everyday use, such as newspapers, street signs, or casual writing, Hebrew is often written without Nikud. However, learning it is essential for beginners to grasp pronunciation and comprehend the language's structure more deeply, so we will be utilizing it extensively in this series. As you progress in your Hebrew studies, the reliance on Nikud will certainly lessen. Think of it as training wheels, which once removed, will find you cycling smoothly through the language.

From Right to Left

The reason behind Hebrew's right-to-left orientation has been debated for decades. One theory suggests that this writing style evolved from the methods used in ancient times for inscribing text onto stone tablets. It's believed that a right-handed person, who would typically hold a chisel in their left hand and a hammer in their right, would find it more natural to inscribe from right to left. This would prevent their hand from obstructing the text and make the process of carving on stone more efficient and comfortable.

Imagine English sentences as if they were reflected in a mirror. For instance, the word "peace" would appear as "ecaep." Shalom would appear as the following:

---

[1] The sounds they make can be referenced on page ____.

```
        O
 " M L SH "
        A
   <------
```

This visual trick can help you practice the mental shift needed for Hebrew. It's not just about reading the letters in reverse order; it's about training your brain to start from the right and move leftward seamlessly. Try reading these mirror-reflected English words: "evol", "gninrael", "gnikool".

Despite this directional shift, Hebrew maintains a familiarity with linearity and shares the same punctuation rules as English. Periods, commas, and question marks – all these are used in the same way, just placed at the opposite end of the sentence.

Transliteration

Transliteration is the process of converting text from one writing system into another while trying to maintain the phonetic characteristics of the original language. In the context of learning Hebrew, this involves representing Hebrew sounds using our alphabet.

The following table will include a key for the pronunciation of every Hebrew letter and vowel we will use. It's designed to guide you in pronouncing Hebrew words correctly, even before you become fully comfortable with the Hebrew script. For instance, the Hebrew letter 'ב' can be transliterated as 'b' or 'v', depending on its usage in a word.

The Nikud is particularly important to understand because it ultimately dictates how a word is pronounced. The closest comparison to Hebrew vowel sounds is found in Spanish. In both languages, vowels tend to have consistent and distinct sounds: *a* (ah), *e* (eh), *i* (ee), *o* (oh), *and u* (oo). For example:

- 'אָ' (*kamatz*) sounds like the 'a' in "father".

- **'אֵ'** (*tsere*) is similar to the 'e' in "they".

- **'אִ'** (*chirik*) resembles the 'ee' in "see" or the 'i' in the Spanish word "si".

- **'אוֹ'** (*cholam*) is akin to the 'o' in "no".

- **'אוּ'** (*shuruk*) sounds like the 'oo' in "food".

These examples are not perfect equivalents but serve as a helpful starting point. As you progress, the goal is to transition from relying on transliterations to reading and understanding Hebrew in its native script.

We will not learn the names of the vowels, but only how to identify and use them correctly.

A note: this table does not encompass every single sound found in the Hebrew language. For instance, while Hebrew does have a phonetic equivalent to the 'J' sound in English, as in "jump," this sound is not prevalent in standard Hebrew and is typically seen in loanwords or specific dialects. As such, it won't be included in our initial transliteration guide.

The goal of this approach is to streamline your learning process by introducing the most fundamental and frequently used sounds first. Once you have mastered these core sounds and the basic structure of the language, you can gradually expand your knowledge to include more complex and less common phonetic elements.

Name of Letter	Transliterated	Sound	Consonants	Name of Vowel	Transliterated	Sound	Nikud
alef	---	.	א	shva nach		STOP	טְ

vet	v	[v]	בּ
bet	b	[b]	בּ
gimel	g	[g]	ג
dalet	d	[d]	ד
he	h	[h]	ה
vav	v	[v]	ו
zayin	z	[z]	ז
chet	ch	[χ]	ח
tet	t	[t]	ט
yod	y	[y]	י
khaf, khaf sofit	kh	[c]	כ ך
kaf	c, k	[k]	כּ
lamed	l	[l]	ל
mem, mem sofit	m	[m]	מ ם

chataf patach			חֲ
chataf kamatz	a	ah	חֳ
patach			טַ
kamatz			טָ
tzeire			טֵ
segol	e	eh	טֶ
chataf segol			חֱ
chirik	i	ee	טִ
chirik male			טִי
cholam	o	oh	טֹ
cholam male			טוֹ
kubutz	u	oo	טֻ
shuruk			טוּ

nun, nun sofit	n	[n]	נ ן
samech	s	[s]	ס
ayin	---	-	ע
fei, fei sofit	f	[f]	פ ף
pei	p	[p]	פ
tzadi, tzadi sofit	tz, ts	[ts]	צ ץ
kuf	c, k	[k]	ק
reish	r, rr	[r]	ר
shin	sh	[sh]	שׁ
sin	s	[s]	שׂ
tav	t	[t]	ת

Chapter Summary

This chapter established the essential foundations for beginning your Hebrew learning journey:

→ **Nikud**: You learned about 'Nikud', the system of dots and dashes that indicate vowels in Hebrew. This is important for our learning process because of Hebrew's consonantal nature and the absence of vowels in traditional writing.

→ **Right-to-Left Reading:** We looked at the unique aspect of Hebrew being read and written from right to left. This included exercises to help you adapt to this directional change.

→ **Phonetics**: You were introduced to the process of transliteration, which involves representing Hebrew sounds using the Latin alphabet.

Practice

Exercise 1:

Match the consonant sound with the Hebrew letter:

1	Q		ב	A
2	B		ל	B
3	L		ט	C
4	P		ק	D
5	T		פ	E
6	R		ר	F

Exercise 2:

Match the vowel sound with the Hebrew vowel (some vowels may have multiple forms!):

1	**Ah**	אִי	A
2	**Eh**	אָ	B
3	**Oh**	אֳ	C
4	**OO**	אִ	D

5	**Eh**	אֶ	E
6	**EE**	אִו	F
7	**OO**	אִו·	G
8	**(stop)**	אֶ	H

Exercise 3:

Write out how this word is meant to sound (backwards Nikud exercise):

O
" M L SH "
A

_____

" T B SH "
A   A

_____

" K ᴜ N H "
A   A

_____

" D V D "
EE A

_____

_____

"T R V I"

EE   EE

O

"H R T"

A

_____

Chapter 1 Answer Key

Exercise 1:

No.	Answer
1	D
2	A
3	B
4	E
5	C
6	F

Exercise 2:

No.	Answer
1	B
2	E or H
3	F
4	C or G
5	E or H

6	A
7	C o G
8	D

Exercise 3:

No.	Answer
1	shalom
2	shabbat
3	hanuka
4	daveed
5	ivrit (Hebrew in Hebrew)
6	torah

Coming up...

In the next chapter, we will dive into learning the Hebrew letters themselves, beginning with the first letter, *alef*. Alef, two vowel sounds, and several consonants will be the focus of the chapter.

Chapter 2 – Basics I: Alef, Consonants, EH, and AH

The limits of my language are the limits of my world.

גְּבוּלוֹת הַשָּׂפָה הֵם גְּבוּלוֹת עוֹלָמִי.

~ Wittgenstein|וִיטְגֶּנְשְׁטֵיין

Each chapter introduces a couple of key grammatical concepts, letters, and vowels, if relevant. This first chapter solely covers our first letters and vowels. Specifically, six Hebrew letters: א (Alef), ג (Gimel), ד (Dalet), ז (Zayin), ט (Tet), and ל (Lamed), along with two basic vowels: EH and AH.

When you encounter each new letter and vowel, take time to try to say the words and sounds out loud. Practice is vital for internalizing the sounds and getting comfortable with pronunciation.

Repetition is key; the more you practice, the better. At the end of the chapter, there will be a quiz and an answer key to review the material thoroughly.

The letters and vowels that we will review (everything in the table below):

Name of Letter	Transliterated	Sound	Consonants	Name of Vowel	Transliterated	Sound	Nikud
alef	---	---	א	chataf patach			אֲ
gimel	g	[g]	ג	chataf kamatz			אֳ
dalet	d	[d]	ד	patach	a	ah	אַ
zayin	z	[z]	ז	kamatz			אָ
tet	t	[t]	ט	tzeire	e	eh	אֵ

lamed	l	[l]	ל		segol	אֶ
					chataf segol	אֱ

First things first - the first letter of the *alef bet* - Alef!

Note: *Like English, there are many fonts and styles of writing Hebrew letters:*

אבבגדהוזחטיכךלמם
נןסעפפףצץקרשׂשׁת

אבבגדהוזחטיככדלמסנוס
עפֶּפֿףצקרשׁשׁת

אבבגדהוזחטיככרלמסנוס
עפֶּפֿףצץקרשטת

אבבגדהוזחטיבעדלמסנוס
עפֿפֿצצץקרשׁשׁת

Alef

Alef (א) is the first letter, and **unlike other consonants, Alef technically does not have its own sound**. It acts as a placeholder for vowel sounds. When pronounced, the sound of Alef is determined by the accompanying vowel.

The letter is generally attributed to representing an ox in ancient Hebrew. It looks somewhat like an 'X' and is unique as it generally doesn't have a sound of its own. Imagine an 'X' marking a silent spot. Or a quiet ox with two horns.

To write Alef in block style:

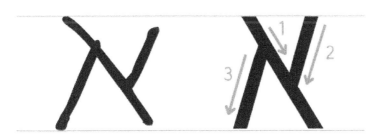

Practice: Write several iterations of *alef* below, from right to left. If you need to, practice more on your own so that you feel comfortable with the look and feel of writing the letter.

א   א   א

Sounds: EH and AH

In Hebrew, vowels are how we know which way the letters are pronounced. Vowels are called "*tnu'ot*" (תנועות), which is the word for *movements*. We can imagine that consonants are static beings that do not know where to go. The vowels, then, tell us in which "direction" to "move" the consonants.

Similarly, in English, the letter "G" does not make a sound, except for the mute and static "ggg" sound. Adding a vowel moves the "G" forward, producing a word and sentence.

The two first "movements" we will learn are "AH" and "EH".

Note: As aforementioned, we will *not* learn the differences between the several vowel markings, but only which marking (Nikud) produces which basic *sound*. Below are several *Nikud* versions for two basic sounds: EH and AH.

In Hebrew, the AH sound is commonly represented by three vowel signs: אָ and אַ

- *Patach* (פַּתח): A single horizontal line under a letter.

- *Kamatz* (קָמץ): A small T-like shape under a letter.

- *Kamatz Katan* (קָמץ קָטָן): Less common, visually identical to Kamatz but sometimes used differently.

The EH sound is represented mainly by two vowel signs: אֱ and אֵ

- *Tsere* (צֵרִי): Two horizontal dots side by side under a letter.

- *Segol* (סֶגוֹל): Three dots arranged in an upside-down triangle under a letter.

Short Practice (א):

Try pronouncing these combinations to get familiar with the AH and EH sounds in Hebrew. Write out the sound that corresponds with that vowel:

אָ - _____   אֵ - _____

אֶ - _____   אֱ - _____

Note: In addition, there are אֱ and אֲ These vowels are similar, with two extra dots underneath, adjacent to the "EH" and "AH" vowels. For the purposes of this guidebook, we can treat them as regular "EH" and "AH" vowels. Their use will be touched on when we introduce the *shva* vowel (אְ).

Introduction to Consonants

In the following, we will cover five consonants. Buckle up!

Gimel

Gimel (ג) is the third letter in the Hebrew alphabet and is pronounced like the 'g' in "go" or "garden."

It has a hard, guttural sound that is consistent and does not change regardless of the vowels accompanying it.

Traditionally, Gimel has symbolized a "benefactor" - someone who gives to others. This is derived from the word "gomel" (גומל), which means the giving of a reward or punishment.

Picture Gimel as a person with open arms, ready to give or embrace. This form reminds you of the 'G' sound in "giving."

To write Gimel in block style:

Dalet

Dalet $(\daleth)$ is the fourth letter in the Hebrew alphabet, pronounced like the 'd' in "door" or "day." In fact, it traditionally comes from the word for "door" - *delet* (דלת). It can symbolize a gateway from one state of being to another. The pictograph looks somewhat like a closed tent door.

Associate the 'D' sound with a door slightly open (symbolizing an invitation or a pathway).

To write Dalet in block style:

Practice: Write several iterations of *gimel* and *dalet* below, from right to left.

Practice: Below is a list of several combinations of Hebrew letters and vowels, with an emphasis on **gimel** and **dalet**. Try to pronounce the written letters on the right *without* looking at the transliteration on the left. You can check yourself by looking at the transliteration as you progress.

Pronunciation	**Hebrew Syllable**
'ahg'	אַג
'gahd'	גָד
'dahg'	דַג
'ahd'	אָד
'ehg'	אֶג
'geh-d'	גֶד
'dehg'	דֶג
'ehd'	אֶד
'ah-gahd'	אַגָד
'eh-gehd'	אֶגֶד
'eh-gahd'	אֶגָד
'ah-dehg'	אַדֶג

Zayin

Zayin (ז) is the seventh letter in the Hebrew alphabet, pronounced like the 'z' in "zebra" or "zoo." It has a buzzing, vibrant sound that is straightforward and consistent across different words. It might have originally represented an agricultural implement like a mattock or plow, with meanings like "harvest," "food," and "cut."

Zayin resembles a sword or a lightning bolt. Visualize a 'Z'-shaped sword or a striking lightning bolt, symbolizing sharpness and swiftness.

How to write Zayin in block style:

Practice: Write several iterations of *zayin* below, from right to left.

Practice: Below is a combined list of Hebrew letters and vowels, with an emphasis on **zayin**. Pronounce the written letters on the right *without* using the transliteration on the left. After, check yourself by looking at the transliteration as you progress.

Pronunciation	Hebrew Syllable
'zahg'	זַג
'dehz'	דֶז
'ehz'	אֶז
'gah-zahl'	גְזַל
'zehd'	זֶד
'zah-ehl'	זָאֶל
'deh-zeg'	דֶזֶג
'gehz-ar'	גֶזַר

Tet

Tet (ט) is the ninth letter in the Hebrew alphabet. It is pronounced like the 't' in "tall" or "time." It is possible that Tet is related to a Phoenician letter meaning "wheel." It is certainly shaped like a vessel that could contain something good within.

Imagine Tet as a coiled snake in a basket, or a round vessel holding treasure. The 'T' sound can remind you of the hidden treasures within.

To write Tet in block style:

Practice: Write several iterations of *tet* below, from right to left.

_____   _____   ט   ט   ט

_____   _____   _____   _____   _____   _____

Practice: Below is a combined list of Hebrew letters and vowels, with an emphasis on **tet**. Pronounce the written letters on the right *without* using the transliteration on the left. After, check yourself by looking at the transliteration as you progress.

Pronunciation	Hebrew Syllable
'tahz'	טַז
'deht'	טֵד
'eht'	אֵט
'gaht-ahl'	גָטַל
'tehd'	טֶד

Pronunciation	Hebrew Syllable
'ahtz-ehd'	אַטְזֶד
'tah-ehl'	טָאֶל
'deh-tez'	דֶטֶז
'geht-ar'	גֶטַר

Lamed

Lamed (ל) is the twelfth letter in the Hebrew alphabet, pronounced like the 'l' in "lion" or "lamp." Lamed likely originated from the representation of an ox-goad or a shepherd's crook. The name comes from the root *lamad* (ד-מ-ל), meaning to learn or teach. It could be imagined as a staff, used to prick, sting, or incite - as a shepherd might prod cattle!

To write Lamed in block style:

Practice: Write several iterations of *lamed* below, from right to left.

_____   _____   ל   ל   ל

___   ___   ___   ___   ___   ___   ___   ___   ___   ___   ___   ___

Practice: Below is a combined list of Hebrew letters and vowels, with an emphasis on **lamed**. Pronounce the written letters on the right *without* using the transliteration on the left. After, check yourself by looking at the transliteration as you progress.

Pronunciation	Hebrew Word
'lahz'	לַז
'dehl'	דֶל
'ehl'	אֶל
'gah-laht'	גָלַט
'lehd'	לֶד
'ahl-tehz'	אַלְטֶז
'lah-eht'	לָאֶט
'deh-lez'	דְלֶז
'geh-lar'	גֶלַר

Chapter Summary

→ **Introduction to Key Hebrew Letters**: In this chapter, we embarked on our Hebrew language journey by exploring six fundamental letters: א (Alef), ג (Gimel), ד (Dalet), ז (Zayin), ט (Tet), and ל (Lamed). We focused on:

- **Learning to Write**: Gaining familiarity with how to write these letters.
- **Understanding Pronunciation**: Delving into the unique sounds each letter represents and practicing their pronunciation.

→ **Developing Hebrew Language Skills**:

- **Engaging in Practice**: Through exercises, you are beginning to strengthen your Hebrew abilities.
- **Emphasizing Repetition**: Keep it up!

Consistent practice is key to mastering these foundational aspects of the Hebrew language. Ensure you follow the exercises provided and create a regular practice schedule. This will greatly aid in developing a deeper understanding and familiarity with the Hebrew letters introduced in this chapter.

Practice

Exercise 1:

Match each transliteration number on the far right with the corresponding Hebrew syllable on the right. Draw a line or write the letter next to the number to indicate the match. Note that some transliterations may have similar sounds, but different Nikud signifies different vowel sounds.

	Transliteration		Hebrew	
1	gad		לֵאג	A
2	dag		זַג	B
3	gez		גֶז	C
4	zag		גַד	D
5	leg		זֵג	E

Exercise 2:

Fill in the blank with the transliterated sound that is missing. Identify the Hebrew consonant and vowel. Refer back to the takeaways from this chapter if you are stuck!

No.	Pronunciation	Hebrew word with Nikud
Ex.	[dag]	דָג
1	[ge____]	גֶטל

2	[a_____]	אָזֶל
3	[_____l]	זַאל
4	[de_____]	דְּלֶזֶל
5	[ze_____]	זְטֶל

Exercise 3:

Below, write the corresponding Hebrew word based on the transliteration provided.

Note: There is no need to write the vowels. This practice is solely for writing Hebrew letters.

No.	Transliteration	Hebrew Word
1	Gez	_____
2	Agad	_____
3	Get	_____
4	Ta'al	_____
5	Ted	_____
6	Galet	_____
7	Gadel	_____

Chapter 2 Answer Key

Exercise 1:

No.	Answer
1	D
2	E
3	C
4	B
5	A

Exercise 2:

No.	Answer
1	getel
2	azel
3	za'al
4	delezel
5	zetel

Exercise 3:

No.	Answer
1	גז
2	אגד
3	גט
4	תאל
5	טד
6	גלט
7	טדל

Coming up...

In the next chapter, we will continue to build on this foundation by introducing additional "regular" letters, doubling the number of consonants you know, before we move on to more complex and special letters.

Chapter 3 – Basics II: More Consonants

Language is the dress of thought.

שָׂפָה הִיא הֶרְגֵּל הַמַּחְשָׁבָה.

~ Samuel Johnson‏סָמוּאֶל גֹ'ונְסוֹן

Language shapes our understanding of the world. We continue to build our basic Hebrew reading, writing, and pronouncing skills by covering more consonants.

This chapter will guide you through Mem, Nun, Samekh, Qof, Resh, Tsade, and Tav. Let's continue one letter at a time; by the end of this, we will be able to begin practicing with relevant real Hebrew words. Let the world of Hebrew unfolds before you.

Letters and vowels that we will be covering (highlighted):

Name of Letter	Transliterated	Sound	Consonants	Name of Vowel	Transliterated	Sound	Nikud
alef	---	---	א	chataf patach			אֲ
gimel	g	[g]	ג	chataf kamatz	a	ah	אֳ
dalet	d	[d]	ד	patach			אַ
zayin	z	[z]	ז	kamatz			אָ
tet	t	[t]	ט	tzeire	e	eh	אֵ
lamed	l	[l]	ל	segol			אֶ

mem	m	[m]	מ	chataf segol		אֱ
nun	n	[n]	נ			
samech	s	[s]	ס			
tzadi	tz, ts	[ts]	צ			
quf	k	[k]	ק			
reish	r, rr	[r]	ר			
tav	t, th	[t]	ת			

Mem

Mem (מ) is the thirteenth letter of the Hebrew alphabet, pronounced like the 'm' in "moon" or "mother." It is attributed to the meaning of water, and likely originated from the Egyptian hieroglyph for water, which was adapted into the Phoenician alphabet. Mem resembles waves in the ocean. Think of the 'M' sound as the murmur of waves, linking the sound and shape to the concept of water.

To write Mem in block style:

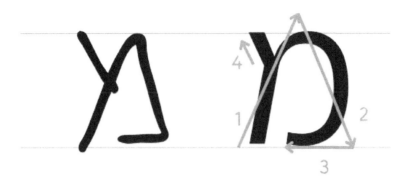

Practice: Write several iterations of *mem* below.

_____   _____   מ   מ   מ

_____   _____   _____   _____   _____   _____

Practice: Below is a combined list of Hebrew letters and vowels, with an emphasis on **mem**. Try to pronounce the written letters on the right *without* using the transliteration on the left.

Pronunciation	Hebrew Syllable
'mahz'	מַז
'gah-mahl'	גָּמַל
'mehd'	מֵד
'mah-eht'	מָאֶט
'deh-mez'	דֶמֶז

Pronunciation	Hebrew Syllable
'gehm-ar'	גֶּמַר

Nun

Nun (נ) is the fourteenth letter in the Hebrew alphabet, pronounced like the 'n' in "night" or "noon."

It probably evolved from a Phoenician symbol for a fish or a snake. In ancient Semitic languages, Nun represents fish or continuity. Nun can be visualized as a bent fishhook. The 'N' sound can be associated with a fish swimming in water.

To write Nun in block style:

Practice: Write several iterations of *nun* below, from right to left.

נ   נ   נ

Practice: Below is a combined list of Hebrew letters and vowels, with an emphasis on **nun**. Try to pronounce the written letters on the right *without* using the transliteration on the left.

Pronunciation	Hebrew Syllable
'nahz'	נַז
'gah-nahl'	גָּנָל
'neh-d'	נֶד
'nah-eht'	נָאֶט
'deh-nez'	דֶּנֶז
'gehn-ar'	גֶּנַר

Samekh

Samekh (ס) is the fifteenth letter in the Hebrew alphabet, pronounced like the 's' in "sun" or "snake."

It might have originated from the Egyptian hieroglyph for a pillar. Samekh symbolizes support or protection in ancient Semitic scripts. Imagine Samekh as a shield or a supportive pillar.

To write Samekh in block style:

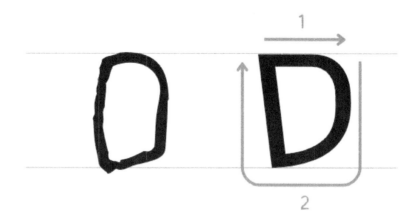

Practice: Write several iterations of *Samekh* below.

_____ _____   ס   ס   ס

_____ _____ _____ _____ _____ _____

Practice: Below is a combined list of Hebrew letters and vowels, with an emphasis on **samekh**. Try to pronounce the written letters on the right *without* using the transliteration on the left.

Pronunciation	Hebrew Syllable
'sahz'	סַז
'dehs'	זֶס
'ehs'	אֶס
'gah-sahl'	גָסַל
'sehd'	סֶד
'sah-eht'	סָאֶט
'deh-set'	זֶסֶט
'gehs-ar'	גֶסַר

Qof

Qof $\left(\boxed{\text{ק}}\right)$ is the nineteenth letter in the Hebrew alphabet, pronounced like the 'k' in "kite" but deeper in the throat, similar to the Arabic 'Qaf'. In transliterating the sound, we will use either *q* or *k*.

To write Qof in block style:

Practice: Write several iterations of *Qof* below.

ק   ק   ק

Practice: Below is a combined list of Hebrew letters and vowels, with an emphasis on **Qof**. Try to pronounce the written letters on the right *without* using the transliteration on the left.

Pronunciation	Hebrew Syllable
'kahz'	קֹז
'dehk'	דֵק
'ehk'	אֶק

Pronunciation	Hebrew Syllable
'gah-kahl'	גָּקָל
'keh-d'	קֶד
'kah-eht'	קָאֶט
'deh-keg'	דֶּקֶג
'geh-kar'	גֶּקַר

Resh

Resh (ר) is the twentieth letter in the Hebrew alphabet, pronounced like the 'r' in "rose" or "red."

This sound is a rolling or trilled 'r', distinct from the English 'r'. It may have evolved from a head or a person's profile in ancient scripts. Thus, Resh represents a head, leader, or beginning in various Semitic languages. In fact, the word *rosh* in Hebrew (ראש) is the word for *head*. Resh can be visualized as a bent head or a person in profile.

Note on pronunciation: Different cultures have different ways of pronouncing the letter "R." Modern Hebrew, because of its cross-cultural quality of being affected by people from all over the world, has several methods of pronunciation. Generally, however, the classic American "arr" may be too round for the conventional Hebrew accent. The traditional sound of *resh* borders either on a Spanish sounding "*rrr*", or on a deep, guttural sounding "*grr*".

To write Resh in block style:

Practice: Write several iterations of *Resh* below.

ר   ר   ר

Practice: Below is a combined list of Hebrew letters and vowels, with an emphasis on **Resh**. Try to pronounce the written letters on the right *without* using the transliteration on the left.

Pronunciation	Hebrew Syllable
'rahz'	רַז
'dehr'	דֵּר
'ehr'	אֵר
'gah-rahl'	גָּרַל
'rehd'	רֵד
'rah-eht'	רָאֵט
'deh-rek'	דֶּרֶק

Pronunciation	Hebrew Syllable
'gehr-as'	גְּרַס

Tsade

Tsade (צ), also spelled Tzadi, is the eighteenth letter in the Hebrew alphabet. It's pronounced like the 'ts' in "nuts" or "cats." To the average American ears, the letter may sound like a combination of 't' and 's', producing a new sibilant consonant.

It is thought to have derived from a pictogram of a man on his side, possibly representing a hunter in a lying position. It symbolizes righteousness or faithfulness in ancient Semitic languages. In fact, the Hebrew word for "righteous man" is *tsadik* - (צדיק). Tsade can be envisioned as a person in a prayerful or meditative posture.

To write Tsade in block style:

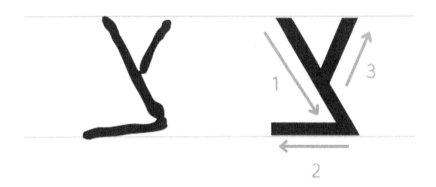

Practice: Write several iterations of *Tsade* below.

Practice: Below is a combined list of Hebrew letters and vowels, with an emphasis on **Tsade**. Try to pronounce the written letters on the right *without* using the transliteration on the left.

Pronunciation	Hebrew Syllable
'tsahz'	צָז
'tsedek'	צֶדֶק
'tzeh'	צֵא
'gah-tsal'	גָּצַל
'tsehd'	צֵד
'tsah-eht'	צָאֵט
'deh-tsek'	דֶּצֵק
'gehts-ar'	גֶּצָר

Tav

Tav (ת) is the twenty-second and final letter of the Hebrew alphabet, pronounced like the 't' in "table" or "time." It likely originated from a mark or a simple cross. For us, Tav could resemble a simple cross or a signpost. The 'T' sound can be associated with marking a spot or making a sign.

Note on pronunciation: In traditional Ashkenazi Hebrew, there is a difference in pronunciation between *Tav* and *Tet*. Tav without a *dagesh* - the dot in the middle of the letter that we will cover later

- was actually considered "*Sav*", and had a hard "sss" sound similar to *Samekh*. Also, the letter has been traditionally translated as "th" as well.

Academics differ on the original sound of spoken *Tav* two thousand years ago. Therefore, modern Hebrew decided to attribute the hard "T" sound to the letter, like *Tet*.

To write Tav in block style:

Practice: Write several iterations of *tav* below.

ת   ת   ת

Practice: Below is a combined list of Hebrew letters and vowels, with an emphasis on **tav**. Try to pronounce the written letters on the right *without* using the transliteration on the left.

Pronunciation	Hebrew Practice
'tahz'	תַז
'deht'	דֶת

Pronunciation	Hebrew Practice
'eht'	אֵת
'gah-tahl'	גָּתַל
'tehd'	תֵּד
'tah-eht'	תָאֵט
'deh-tek'	דֵּתֶק
'geht-ar'	גֵּתַר

Chapter Summary

→ **Further Exploration of Hebrew Consonants**: In this chapter, our journey into the Hebrew language deepened as we introduced seven more consonants: Mem (מ), Nun (נ), Samekh (ס), Qof (ק), Resh (ר), Tsade (צ), and Tav (ת).

Keep practicing and prepare to dive even deeper in the upcoming chapters!

Practice

Exercise 1:

Match the transliteration number (far left column) with the corresponding Hebrew word letter (far right column). Write the letter next to the number to indicate the match.

	Transliteration	**Hebrew Word with Nikud**	
1	Maz	גָּתַר	**A**
2	Mad	נַז	**B**
3	Ma'at	תַּאַט	**C**
4	Damaz	גָּנַל	**D**
5	Gamár	אֶת	**E**
6	Naz	גֶּרֶס	**F**
7	Ganál	דַּנַז	**G**
8	Na'at	גָּמַר	**H**
9	Danáz	צַד	**I**
10	Ganár	דֶּרֶק	**J**
11	Darék	מַאַט	**K**

12	Garés	תַד	L
13	Tzaz	אֶצֵּר	M
14	Etzár	מַז	N
15	Tzad	צַז	O
16	Et	דַתֵק	P
17	Gatal	גַנֵר	Q
18	Tad	גַתֵל	R
19	Ta'at	מַד	S
20	Daték	דַמֵז	T
21	Gatar	נַאֵט	U

Exercise 2:

Read the transliteration provided in the left column. Then, looking at the pair of words in the right column, circle the word that is spelled correctly and matches the transliteration.

	Transliteration	**Hebrew**
1	Gamál	גָמָל / קָמָל

2	Émet	אֱמֶת / אֱסֶת
3	Dékel	דֶקֶל / שׂמֶקֶל
4	Tzél	צֶל / זֶל
5	Dálet	דֶלֶת / דֶרֶת
6	Már	מַר / מָק

Exercise 3:

Fill in the blank with the transliterated sound that is missing. Identify the Hebrew consonant and vowel. Refer back to the takeaways from this chapter if you are stuck!

	Transliteration	Fill in the Missing Letter
1	Gézer	גֶ_ר
2	Degél	דֶ_ל
3	Set	_ֶס
4	Delek	דֶל_
5	Rader	רַ_ר
6	Nes	_ֶנ
7	Mas	ס_

Exercise 4:

For each transliteration listed on the left, write the corresponding Hebrew word in the space provided on the right. Use only the "EH" and "AH" vowel sounds to assist you in recalling the correct Hebrew spelling. Remember, Hebrew is read from right to left.

	Transliteration	**Write the Hebrew Word**
1	Séker	_____
2	Sélek	_____
3	Tzad	_____
4	Set	_____
5	Géder	_____
6	Agad	_____
7	Tzag	_____

Chapter 3 Answer Key

Exercise 1:

No.	Answer
1	N
2	S
3	K
4	T
5	H
6	B
7	D
8	U
9	G
10	Q
11	J
12	F
13	O
14	M

15	I
16	E
17	R
18	L
19	C
20	P
21	A

Exercise 2:

No.	Answer
1	גָּמָל
2	אֱמֶת
3	דֶּקֶל
4	צֵל
5	דֶּלֶת
6	מַר

Exercise 3:

No.	Answer
1	גזר
2	דגל
3	סט
4	דלק
5	רדר
6	נס
7	מס
8	מר

Coming up...

Looking ahead to Chapter 4, we will introduce you to more complex elements of Hebrew: additional vowels and special letters such as He, Vav, and Yud. These are crucial components of the language. Keep practicing, stay curious, and let's continue this together in the next chapter!

Chapter 4 – He, Yud, Vav, OH, EE, OO, and *Shva*

Language structures the relationship between humans.

הַשָּׂפָה בּוֹנָה אֶת כָּל הַיְחָסִים שֶׁבֵּין בְּנֵי אָדָם.

Jacques Lacan|זָ'אק לאקאן ~

In this chapter, we will delve into three significant letters: ה (He), י (Yod), and ו (Vav). In addition to these letters, we will also explore three important vowel sounds: OH, OO, and EE.

Fun fact: One of the reasons that these three letters, ה, י, and ו are special is because they comprise the name of the Jewish God according to ancient Biblical texts. Additionally, they make up the words that have to do with the verb "*to be*". Jewish sages have contemplated the meaning of *being* and *godliness* for ages. As we will learn in Books II and II, the letters ה, ו, and י are sometimes interchangeable in Hebrew. This is evident in various Hebrew words where the substitution of these letters changes the word's meaning but retains a phonetic or conceptual similarity.

Name of Letter	Transliterated	Sound	Consonants	Name of Vowel	Transliterated	Sound	Nikud
alef	---	.	א	chataf patach			חֲ
gimel	g	[g]	ג	chataf kamatz	a	ah	חֳ
dalet	d	[d]	ד	patach			טַ
he	h	[h]	ה	kamatz			טָ

Name	Translit	IPA	Letter
vav	v	[v]	ו
zayin	z	[z]	ז
tet	t	[t]	ט
yod	y	[y]	י
lamed	l	[l]	ל
mem,	m	[m]	מ
nun	n	[n]	נ
samech	s	[s]	ס
tzadi	tz, ts	[ts]	צ
kuf	c, k	[k]	ק
reish	r, rr	[r]	ר
tav	t, th	[t]	ת

Name	Vowel	Sound	Symbol
tzeire			טֵ
segol	e	eh	טֶ
chataf segol			חֱ
chirik	i	ee	טִ
chirik male			טִי
cholam	o	oh	טֹ
cholam male			טוֹ
kubutz	u	oo	טֻ
shuruk			טוּ

He (pronounced "hey")

He (ה) is the fifth letter in the Hebrew alphabet, typically pronounced like the 'h' in "house" or "happy." It produces a soft, breathy sound, often used at the beginning or end of words. It likely originated from a hieroglyph or a pictogram representing a man with raised arms, symbolizing exclamation or revelation. (In other words, *"Hey!!!"*). In Jewish mysticism, *He* is often associated with the divine breath, inspiration, and the feminine aspect of God.

To write He in block style:

Practice: Write several iterations of *He* below.

ה   ה   ה

Pronunciation Note: The letter *He* adds a pronunciation rule to the AH vowels. When there is an AH vowel under a *He* letter - after the vowels EH, OH, or OO - then that vowel applies as a dipthong before the *He*.

As an example, the word *tameah* means "pondering." It is spelled תָּמֶה tah-**me-ah.** The AH vowel underneath the *He* becomes a diphthong with the EH vowel under the *Mem* - in other words, we create an "eyah" or "eh-ah" sound. This rule applies to the letters *Ayin* and *Het* as well, and we will explore this later.

Practice: Below is a combined list of Hebrew letters and vowels, with an emphasis on **He.** Try to pronounce the written letters on the right *without* using the transliteration on the left.

Pronunciation	Hebrew Syllable
'hahz'	הַז
'deh'	דֶּה
'eh'	אֶה
'gah-hahl'	גָּהַל
'hehd'	הֵד
'hah-eht'	הָאֶט
'deh-hek'	דֶּהֶק
'geh-har'	גֶּהַר

Yud

Yod (י) is the tenth letter in the Hebrew alphabet, typically pronounced like the 'y' in "yes" or "yoga."

It may have originated from a pictogram of an extended hand or arm, and it may represent a work or a deed. Traditionally, Yod has been envisioned as a hand or an extended finger.

Fun Fact: Yod is the smallest letter in the Hebrew alphabet but has significant mystical importance. It represents the omnipresent, all-encompassing nature of God.

To write Yod in block style:

Practice: Write several iterations of *yod* below.

_____

_____   _____   ı   ı   ı

_____

_____   _____   _____   _____   _____   _____

Practice: Below is a combined list of Hebrew letters and vowels, with an emphasis on **yod**. Try to pronounce the written letters on the right *without* using the transliteration on the left.

Pronunciation	Hebrew Syllable
'yahz'	יַז
'gah-yahl'	גַּיְל
'yehd'	יֶד
'yah-eht'	יָאֵט
'dey-ek'	דֶּיֶק
'gey-ar'	גֶּיַר

Vav

Vav (**ו**) is the sixth letter in the Hebrew alphabet. As a consonant, it's pronounced like the 'v' in "vase" or "vote." Vav is versatile, also serving as a vowel marker in certain contexts. It probably evolved from a pictogram of a peg or hook. The 'V' sound can be linked with the firmness and simplicity of a peg or nail.

Fun Fact: Vav is known as the "connector" in the Hebrew language, often used as a conjunction (namely, the English word *and*). It also represents the number six and symbolizes connection and continuity.

To write Vav in block style:

Practice: Write several iterations of *Vav* below.

Vowels: EE, OH, and OO

We now venture into the nuanced realm of EE, OH, OO. The EE sound resonates with a clear, long 'ee' as in "bee." The OH sound is like the 'oh' of "show." The OO sound sounds like 'oo' in "food."

The EE sound is represented by two forms: **אֱ** and **אִי**

The OH sound is represented by אֹ and אוֹ

The OO sound is represented by אֻ and אוּ

Practice: Below is a combined list of Hebrew letters and vowels, with an emphasis on **OH, OO,** and **EE**. Try to pronounce the written letters on the right *without* using the transliteration on the left.

Transliteration	**Hebrew Word**
layil *(night)*	לַיִל
rut *(Ruth)*	רוּת
daveed *(David)*	דָּוִד
torah *(Torah)*	תּוֹרָה
dor *(generation)*	דּוֹר
yadid *(friend)*	יָדִיד
golah *(exile)*	גּוֹלָה
tahor *(pure)*	טָהוֹר
moreh *(teacher)*	מוֹרֶה
sirah *(boat)*	סִירָה
kool *("cool")*	קוּל

zikah (*passion*)   זִיקָה

ra'ui (*worthy*)   רָאוּי

toda (*"thank you"*)   תּוֹדָה

notzah (*feather*)   נוֹצָה

Chapter Summary

→ **Exploring Key Hebrew Letters and Vowels**: This chapter delved into three Hebrew letters: ה (He), י (Yod), and ו (Vav), alongside the vowel sounds OH, EE, and OO. Key focus areas included:

- We explored how these letters function in various word constructions and their role in producing specific vowel sounds.
- The chapter offered a range of exercises to practice writing, reading, and pronouncing Hebrew words, emphasizing the use of ה (He), י (Yod), and ו (Vav), and the vowels OH, EE, and OO.
- The chapter provided insights into the versatile roles of ה (He), י (Yod), and ו (Vav) in Hebrew grammar.

Practice

Exercise 1:

For each numbered Hebrew word with Nikud, write out the correct transliteration.

	Correct Option	**Hebrew Word with Nikud**
1		זַיִת
2		וִינָה
3		הוֹרָה
4		גָּדוֹל
5		גִּידוּל
6		נוֹרָא
7		מוֹרָה
8		לַיְלָה
9		יָד
10		רוֹאֶה
11		קוֹל
12		צוֹדֵק

13		נֹאד
14		לִימוּד
15		מוּסָר
16		תוֹרָה

Exercise 2:

For each Hebrew word with Nikud on the right, complete the missing syllable in the transliteration provided in the middle column.

	Transliteration	Hebrew Word with Nikud
Ex.	[ro-**ded**]	רוֹדֵד
1	[za-____]	זָרָה
2	[ti-____]	טִירָה
3	[da-____]	דָּלִיק
4	[____-il]	גִּיל
5	[so-____]	סוֹדִי

6	[no-____]	נוֹרָא
7	[kiyu-____]	קִיּוּמִי
8	[mi-____]	מִלָּה
9	[ya-ri-____]	יָרִיתִי
10	[ra-____-nu]	רָצִינוּ
11	[di-____]	דִּינָה
12	[ni-____-na]	נִצְנָה
13	[____-ir]	סִיר
14	[tu-____-ai]	טוּרָאי
15	[li-____]	לִירוֹת
16	[ri-____]	רִינָה
17	[da-____]	דָּנִי

18	[ma-____]	מָנָה
19	[mo-____]	מוֹדֵל
20	[zo-____]	זוֹרֵק
21	[____-uk]	צוּק
22	[do-____]	דוֹדָה

Exercise 3:

For each transliteration given in the left column, write the corresponding Hebrew word in the space provided on the right. Use your knowledge of Hebrew sounds and spelling rules to determine the correct Hebrew letters. Remember that Hebrew is read and written from right to left.

	Transliteration	**Write the Hebrew Word**
1	Ronit	_____
2	Tali	_____
3	Ana	_____
4	David	_____

5	Daniel	_____
6	Yannai	_____
7	Danah	_____
8	Lanah	_____
9	Tedi	_____
10	Dani	_____
11	Dor	_____
12	Dudi	_____
13	Yoni	_____
14	Eyal	_____

Chapter 4 Answer Key

Exercise 1:

No.	Answer
1	Zayit
2	Vinah
3	Horah
4	Gadol
5	Gidul
6	Norah
7	Morah
8	Laylah
9	Yad
10	Ro'eh
11	Kol
12	Tzodek
13	Nad
14	Limud

15	Musar
16	Torah

Exercise 2:

No.	Answer
1	za-**ra**
2	ti-**ra**
3	da-**lik**
4	**g**il
5	so-**di**
6	no-**ra**
7	kiyu-**mi**
8	mi-**la**
9	ya-ri-**ti**
10	ra-**tsi**-nu

11	di-**na**
12	ni-**tsa**-na
13	**s**ir [see-r]
14	tu-**r**ai
15	li-**rot**
16	ri-**na**
17	**da**-ni
18	ma-**na**
19	mo-**del**
20	zo-**rek**
21	**ts**uk
22	**do**-da

Exercise 3:

No.	Answer

1	רונית
2	טלי
3	אנה
4	דוד
5	דניאל
6	ינאי
7	דנה
8	לנה
9	טדי
10	דני
11	דור
12	דודי
13	יוני
14	אייל

Coming up...

In the next chapter, Chapter 5, we will be introducing the final forms of some consonants: ם and ן.

Chapter 5 – 'Ending' Letters, Male and Female, and Plurals

You don't live in a country; you live in a language.

לֹא בַּמְדִינָה אַתָּה גָּר אֶלָּא בַּשָׂפָה.

– Emil Cioran|ואראן'צ אֱמִיל

Hebrew differs greatly from English in its approach to gender and plurality. Unlike English's relatively simple 's' for plurals, Hebrew uses different endings for masculine and feminine nouns. Additionally, the concept of 'ending' letters, where certain consonants change form at the end of words, is unique to semitic languages like Hebrew and Arabic.

In this chapter, we will explore these aspects step-by-step. You'll learn about the 'ending' letters ם and ן (Mem Sofit and Nun Sofit).

- In Hebrew, there are five letters that have distinct final forms: Kaf (ך), Mem (ם), Nun (ן), Pe (ף), and Tsadi (ץ). These are known as אותיות סופיות (final letters or "Sofit" letters).
- These final forms are used exclusively at the end of words.

Letters and vowels that we will cover in this chapter (highlighted):

Name of Letter	Transliterated	Sound	Consonants	Name of Vowel	Transliterated	Sound	Nikud
alef	---	.	א	chataf patach			חֲ
gimel	g	[g]	ג	chataf kamatz	a	ah	חֳ
dalet	d	[d]	ד	patach			טַ

he	h	[h]	ה	kamatz			טָ
vav	v	[v]	ו	tzeire			טֵ
zayin	z	[z]	ז	segol	e	eh	טֶ
tet	t	[t]	ט	chataf segol			חֱ
yod	y	[y]	י	chirik			טִ
lamed	l	[l]	ל	chirik male	i	ee	טִי
mem, **mem sofit**	m	[m]	מ ם	cholam			טֹ
nun, **nun sofit**	n	[n]	נ ן	cholam male	o	oh	טוֹ
samech	s	[s]	ס	kubutz			טֻ
tzadi,	tz, ts	[ts]	צ	shuruk	u	oo	טוּ
kuf	c, k	[k]	ק				
reish	r, rr	[r]	ר				
tav	t	[t]	ת				

Let's dive in!

Mem Sofit, Nun Sofit

Mem Sofit

Mem Sofit (ם) is the final form of the letter Mem (מ). It's pronounced exactly the same as the regular Mem, like the 'm' in "moon" or "moment." This ending version of Mem only appears at the end of words, maintaining the same sound but with a distinct shape. You can think of Mem Sofit as a closed or final wave, marking the end of the flow in a word. The shape can remind you of a wave curling over as it reaches the shore.

To write Mem Sofit in block style:

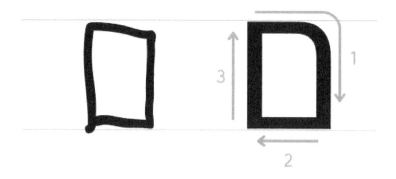

Practice: Write several iterations of *Mem Sofit* below.

Practice: Below is a combined list of Hebrew letters and vowels, with an emphasis on **Mem Sofit**. Try to pronounce the written letters on the right *without* using the transliteration on the left.

Pronunciation	Hebrew Word
'ram'	רַם
'gam'	גַּם
'tam'	תָּם
'deem'	דִים
'om'	עֹם
'nem'	נֶם
'lem'	לְם
'tzam'	צָם
'yahm'	יַם
'koom'	קוּם
'gih-bo-reem'	גִּבּוֹרִים
'toh-ra-neem'	תּוֹרָנִים
'ah-nah-keem'	עֲנָקִים

Nun Sofit

Nun Sofit (|) is the final form of the letter Nun (נ). It's pronounced exactly like the regular Nun, similar to the 'n' in "night" or "noon." This ending version of Nun is used exclusively at the end of words, keeping the same sound but with a distinct appearance. Visualize Nun Sofit as a long fish tail, perhaps signifying the end of the swimming path in a word. The elongated form can represent a final stroke or flourish.

To write Nun Sofit in block style:

Practice: Write several iterations of *Nun Sofit* below.

      ———   ——— | | |

      ———   ———   ———   ———   ———   ———

Practice: Below is a combined list of Hebrew letters and vowels, with an emphasis on **Nun Sofit**. Try to pronounce the written letters on the right *without* using the transliteration on the left.

Pronunciation	Hebrew Word
'gan'	גַּן
'rah-kan'	רָקָן
'mi-ton'	מִתּוֹן
'dee-nee'	דִינִי
'ah-zahn'	עָזָן
'kah-ran'	קָרָן
'lay-lahn'	לֵילָן
'tah-yah-ran'	טַיָּרָן
'see-gahn'	סִיגָן

Chapter Summary

→ **Ending Letters**: The unique aspect of semitic languages is the 'ending' letters, or *Sofit* letters. You learned about Mem Sofit (ם) and Nun Sofit (ן), their usage, and practiced writing them. Understanding these final forms, used exclusively at the end of words, is crucial for reading and writing Hebrew accurately.

Revisit the exercises and examples in this chapter to solidify your understanding and prepare for further exploration of the Hebrew language in upcoming chapters.

Practice

Exercise 1:

Look at each Hebrew word in the right column. Write its transliteration in the blank space. Use this exercise to practice your understanding of Hebrew phonetics and script.

#	Transliteration	Hebrew Word
1	_____	מָדוֹן
2	_____	גָּנֶן
3	_____	תָּמָן
4	_____	יָמִין
5	_____	רָמוֹן
6	_____	תְּקוֹן
7	_____	דָּנֶן
8	_____	רַקָּו
9	_____	זְמָן
10	_____	גַּמָד
11	_____	רִימוֹן

12	_____	תָּמָר
13	_____	דִּינָן
14	_____	סִימָן
15	_____	לִימוֹן
16	_____	גַּגָּן
17	_____	יִרְמוֹן
18	_____	דָּרוֹן

Chapter 5 Answer Key

Exercise 1:

No.	Answer
1	madon
2	ganan
3	taman
4	yamin
5	ramon
6	tikon
7	danan
8	rakan
9	ziman
10	gamad
11	rimon
12	tamar
13	dinan
14	siman

15	limon
16	ganan
17	yirmon
18	diron

Coming up...

The next chapter will introduce another layer of depth. Chapter 6 will focus on the hard and soft sounds of certain Hebrew letters: ב (Bet/Vet), פ (Pe/Fe), כ (Kaf/Chaf), and ש (Shin/Sin). This will mark the second-to-last stage of our pronunciation and guide for this book.

Chapter 6 – The Dagesh: Letter Changes

Language is the painting of our thoughts.

שָׂפָה הִיא צִיּוּר הַמַּחְשָׁבָה.

Chapter 6 introduces you to the Dagesh and its fascinating role in altering the sounds of certain Hebrew letters. In Hebrew, a Dagesh is a diacritical mark appearing as a dot inside a letter. It, basically, creates what are known as hard (emphatic) and soft (gentle) sounds. This chapter focuses on the letters בּ (Bet/Vet), פ (Pe/Fe), and כ (Kaf/Chaf) that use the Dagesh to toggle between their hard and soft sounds. Understanding these variations is vital for proper pronunciation and adds a layer of depth to your Hebrew skills. While Dageshes have grammatical purposes that go beyond pronunciation, at this stage, our focus will be on their phonetic impact.

Additionally, we'll explore ש (Shin/Sin), which, although not involving a Dagesh, follows a similar rule for sound change.

Letters and vowels that will be covered (highlighted):

Name of Letter	Transliterated	Sound	Consonants	Name of Vowel	Transliterated	Sound	Nikud
alef	---	.	א	shva nach		STOP	טְ
vet	v	[v]	ב	chataf patach			תֱ
bet	b	[b]	בּ	chataf kamatz	a	ah	תֳ
gimel	g	[g]	ג	patach			ט
dalet	d	[d]	ד	kamatz			טָ

he	h	[h]	ה	tzeire			טֵ
vav	v	[v]	ו	segol	e	eh	טֶ
zayin	z	[z]	ז	chataf segol			חֱ
tet	t	[t]	ט	chirik			טִ
yod	y	[y]	י	chirik male	i	ee	טִי
khaf	kh	[c]	כ	cholam			טֹ
kaf	c, k	[k]	כּ	cholam male	o	oh	טוֹ
lamed	l	[l]	ל	kubutz			טֻ
mem, mem sofit	m	[m]	ם מ	shuruk	u	oo	טוּ
nun, nun sofit	n	[n]	ן נ				
samech	s	[s]	ס				
fei	f	[f]	פ				
pei	p	[p]	פּ				
tzadi,	tz, ts	[ts]	צ				
kuf	c, k	[k]	ק				

reish	r, rr	[r]	ר
shin	sh	[sh]	שׁ
sin	s	[s]	שׂ
tav	t	[t]	ת

This is a step-by-step guide. Let's dive in!

The Dagesh, and New Letters

- The dagesh is a diacritical mark in the Hebrew alphabet indicating a change in the pronunciation of a letter.
- **Purpose**: It is used to differentiate between the hard and soft sounds of certain letters (known as Beged Kefet letters: ב, ג, ד, כ, פ, ת).
- **Significance**: The presence or absence of a dagesh alters the sound of the letter, which can change the meaning of words in Hebrew.
- **Example**: As seen with Bet, Pe, and Kaf, the dagesh transforms their pronunciation, impacting the nuances of communication in the Hebrew language.

Hard and soft sounds. Other uses (not as practical for us).

In Hebrew, certain letters can have both hard (emphatic) and soft (gentle) sounds. This variation is largely determined by the presence or absence of a "Dagesh," a diacritical mark that appears as a dot in the center of the letter.

Three letters commonly affected by the Dagesh are ב (Bet), פ (Pe), and כ (Kaf):

1. **Bet (ב)**:

    - Without Dagesh, it's pronounced as 'v' (soft sound), like in "vase" (ב).

- With Dagesh, it's pronounced as 'b' (hard sound), like in "book" (בּ).

2. **Pe (פ)**:

   - Without Dagesh, it's pronounced as 'f' (soft sound), like in "fine" (פ).

   - With Dagesh, it's pronounced as 'p' (hard sound), like in "paper" (פּ).

3. **Kaf (כ)**:

   - Without Dagesh, it's pronounced as 'kh' (soft sound), a guttural sound like the 'ch' in "Bach" (כ).

   - With Dagesh, it's pronounced as 'k' (hard sound), like in "king" (כּ).

Bet and Vet

Bet (בּ) is the second letter in the Hebrew alphabet. It has two distinct pronunciations:

1. **With Dagesh (בּ)**: Pronounced as 'b', like in "book."

2. **Without Dagesh (ב)**: Pronounced as 'v', like in "vase."

Bet is derived from the word for "house" in West Semitic and Egyptian languages. Imagine Bet as a house with a door that can be firm and closed (hard 'B') or slightly open and inviting (soft 'V').

To write Bet in block style:

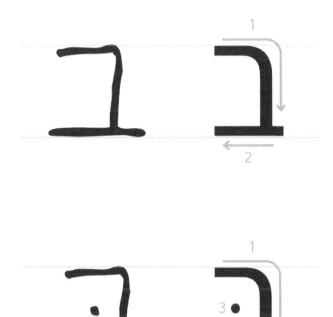

Practice: Write several iterations of *bet* below.

בּ   בּ   בּ

Practice: Below is a combined list of Hebrew letters and vowels, with an emphasis on **Bet/Vet**. Try to pronounce the written letters on the right *without* using the transliteration on the left.

Pronunciation	**Hebrew Word**
'bar'	בַּר

Pronunciation	Hebrew Word
'da-var'	דָּבָר
'tov'	טוֹב
'lev'	לֵב
'bone'	בוהב
'se-viv'	סֶבִיב
'ka-rov'	קָרוֹב

Kaf and Khaf

Kaf (כ) also has two possible sounds:

1. **With Dagesh** (כּ): Pronounced as 'k', similar to the 'k' in "kite" or "king."

2. **Without Dagesh** (כ): Pronounced as 'kh', a guttural sound similar to the 'ch' in the Scottish "loch" or the German "Bach."

Mnemonic: Visualize Kaf as a palm that can either hold something tightly (hard 'K') or gently (soft 'KH').

To write Kaf in block style:

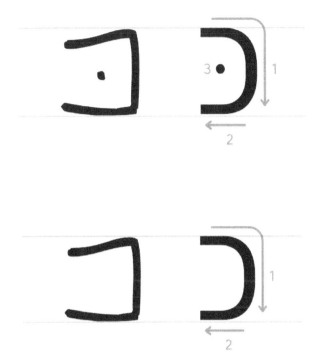

Practice: Write several iterations of *Khaf* below.

                                                           כ   כ   כ

Practice: Below is a combined list of Hebrew letters and vowels, with an emphasis on **Khaf**. Try to pronounce the written letters on the right *without* using the transliteration on the left.

Pronunciation	Hebrew Word
'kar'	כַּר
'mal-lah-kah'	מַלְכָּה

Pronunciation	Hebrew Word
'dee-kah'	דִּיכָא
'kov'	כּוֹב
'ah-khar'	עָכָר
'keel'	כִּיל
'ne-kher'	נֶכֶר
'sa-khan'	סָכַן
'kah-rah'	כָּרָה
'rahk-bah'	רַכְבָּה

Pe and Fe

Pe (פ) is a Hebrew letter with two pronunciations:

- **With Dagesh (פּ)**: Pronounced as 'p', like in "paper" or "pop."

- **Without Dagesh (פ)**: Pronounced as 'f', like in "fine" or "leaf."

The word pe (פה) means mouth - and you can think of the letter Pe as a mouth that can either puff out air forcefully (hard 'P') or softly (soft 'F').

To write Pe in block style:

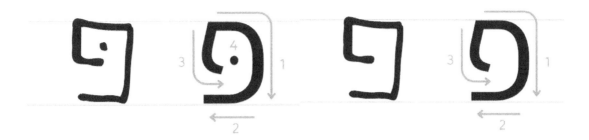

Practice: Write several iterations of *Pe* below.

_____

_____   _____   פ   פ   פ

_____   _____   _____   _____   _____   _____

_____

Practice: Below is a combined list of Hebrew letters and vowels, with an emphasis on **Pe/Fe**. Try to pronounce the written letters on the right *without* using the transliteration on the left.

Pronunciation	Hebrew Word
'par'	פַּר
'ke-feef'	כְּפִיף
'pah-tah'	פָּתָה
'gee-feet'	גִּיפִית
'pol'	פֹּל

Pronunciation	Hebrew Word
'nah-fah'	נָפָה
'raf-sah'	רַפְסָה
'peel'	פִּיל
'se-fer'	סֵפֶר
'poor'	פּוּר

Shin and *Sin*

Not the same rule as the dagesh – still, there are two versions.

Shin (שׁ) is a significant letter in the Hebrew alphabet with two distinct pronunciations based on its position and diacritical marks:

1. **Shin (שׁ)**: When accompanied by a dot on the right side (known as a Shin Dot), it's pronounced 'sh', like in "ship" or "shine."

2. **Sin (שׂ)**: When the dot is on the left side, it becomes Sin and is pronounced 's', like in "sand" or "sister."

The word *shen* (שׁן) means tooth - and indeed the letter looks somewhat like a tooth. You can think of Shin as a tooth that can either be sharp (sound 'SH') or smooth (sound 'S').

To write Shin in block style:

Practice: Write several iterations of *shin* below.

שׁ   שׁ   שׁ

Practice: Below is a combined list of Hebrew letters and vowels, with an emphasis on **Shin/Sin**. Try to pronounce the written letters on the right *without* using the transliteration on the left.

Pronunciation	Hebrew Word
'shalom'	שָׁלוֹם

Pronunciation	Hebrew Word
'mishtah'	מִשְׁתָּה
'gis-hah'	גִּישָׁה
'sheer'	שִׁיר
'ras-kah'	רַשְׁקָה
'shen'	שֵׁן
'ta-sem'	תָּשֵׂם
'sha-ked'	שָׁקֵד
'na-seem'	נָשִׁים
'she-lam'	שְׁלָם

Chapter Summary

➔ **Introduction to Dagesh in Hebrew**: This chapter provided an in-depth understanding of the Dagesh, a diacritical mark in Hebrew that changes the pronunciation of certain letters. While all letters can have a dagesh, only certain letters change their actual sound.

➔ Exploring Hard and Soft Sounds: You learned how the Dagesh affects the letters בּ (Bet/Vet), פ (Pe/Fe), and כ (Kaf/Chaf), altering their sounds between hard (emphatic) and soft (gentle) pronunciations. This variation significantly influences the meaning and nuance of Hebrew words.

This chapter set the stage for the upcoming Chapter 7 - and for the next books in general. After mastering these, you are well on your way to understanding the most difficult pronunciation rules that Hebrew has!

Practice

Exercise 1:

Review each pair of Hebrew words. Identify the correctly spelled word (with the correct Nikud) that matches the provided transliteration. Focus on identifying the subtle differences in Nikud that change the pronunciation and meaning of the words.

Transliteration	Hebrew Word (Correct / Incorrect)	
Davar	דָּבָר / דַּבָּר	1
Tov	טוֹב / טֶב	2
Lev	לֵב / לֶב	3
Saviv	סָבִיב / סַבִּיב	4
Kur	כּוּר / כֶּר	5
Nokhri	נָכְרִי / נַכְּרִי	6
Rakevet	רָכֶבֶת / רַכֶּבֶת	7
Pil	פִּיל / פֵּיל	8
Sefer	סֵפֶר / סֶפֶּר	9
Grafitti	גְרָפִיטִי / גַרְפִּיטִי	10
Kapit	כַּפִּית / כַּפִית	11

Yisrael	יִשְׂרָאֵל / יִשְׂרָאֵל	12
Shlomi	שְׁלוֹמִי / שָׁלוֹמִי	13
Shalom	שָׁלוֹם / שָׁלוֹם	14
Shirutim	שִׁירוּתִים / שִׁירוֹתִים	15
Format	פוֹרמַט / פֶרמַט	16

Exercise 2:

Read each Hebrew word on the right. Complete the transliteration on the left by filling in the missing syllable(s). Focus on the pronunciation and syllable structure of the Hebrew words to find the correct transliteration.

	Transliteration (With Missing Syllable)	**Hebrew Word**
1	Mis-_____	מִסְפָּר
2	Raf-_____-da	רַפְסוֹדָה
3	Mal-_____	מַלְכָּה
4	Pu-_____	פּוּרִים
5	Se-_____	סֵפֶר
6	Pre-_____-um	פְּרֶמְיוּם

7	Bi-_____-ri	בִּיפֹּולָרִי
8	Cho-_____-phy	כֹּורְיֹוגְרַפִּי
9	Ba-_____-ter	בָּרֹומֶטֶר
10	Ze-_____	זֶבְרָה
11	K'vu-_____	קְבוּצָה
12	Le-_____-brek	לְפַבְּרֶק
13	Sh-_____-ti	שְׁרִירוּתִי
14	Sho-_____	שֹׁוקַיִם
15	Sha-_____	שָׁרִי
16	Mish-_____	מִשְׁתָּק
17	Kol ha-a-_____	כָּל הָאֲנָשִׁים

Exercise 3:

Read the transliteration in the middle column. Write the corresponding Hebrew word in the right column. Use the word bank as a reference.

#	Transliteration	Hebrew Word to Fill In
1	Shampoo	_____

2	November	_____
3	Sfaradeet	_____
4	Srokhim	_____
5	Beresheet	_____
6	Midbar	_____
7	Platipus	_____
8	Rosh	_____
9	Sheelah	_____
10	HaSheelah	_____
11	Sha-ilah	_____
12	Yadayim	_____
13	Kulyot	_____
14	Sofer	_____
15	Pitot	_____

Word Bank (with Nikud):

סְפָרְדִית   נוֹבֶמְבֶּר   שַׁמְפוּ   כְּלָיוֹת   יָדַיִם   שְׁאִילָה
מִדְבָּר   בְּרֵאשִׁית   שְׂרוֹכִים   פְּתוֹת   סוֹפֵר
פְּלָטִיפּוּס   רֹאשׁ   שְׁאֵלָה   הַשְּׁאֵלָה

Chapter 6 Answer Key

Exercise 1:

No.	Answer
1	דָּבָר
2	טוֹב
3	לֵב
4	סָבִיב
5	כּוּר
6	נָכְרִי
7	רַכֶּבֶת
8	פִּיל
9	סֵפֶר
10	גְּרַפִּיטִי
11	כַּפִּית
12	יִשְׂרָאֵל

13	שְׁלוֹמִי
14	שָׁלוֹם
15	שִׁירוּתִים
16	פוֹרְמַט

Exercise 2:

No.	Answer
1	mis-**par**
2	raf-**so**-da
3	mal-**ka**
4	pu-**rim**
5	se-**fer**
6	pre-**mi**-yum
7	be-**po-a**-ri
8	kho-**ri-og-ra**-fi
9	ba-**ro-me**-ter
10	ze-**bra**

11	kvu-**tza**
12	le-**fa**-brek
13	sh-**ri**-**ru**-ti
14	sho-**ka**-**yim**
15	sha-**ri**
16	mish-**tak**
17	kol ha-a-**na**-**shim**

Exercise 3:

No.	Answer
1	שַׁמְפּוּ
2	נוֹבֶמְבֶּר
3	סְפָרַדִית
4	שְׂרוֹכִים
5	בְּרֵאשִׁית

6	מִדְבָּר
7	פְּלַטִיפּוּס
8	רֹאשׁ
9	שְׁאֵלָה
10	הַשְׁאֵלָה
11	שְׁאִילָה
12	יָדַיִם
13	כְּלָיוֹת
14	סוֹפֵר
15	פְּתוּתוֹת

Coming up...

Looking ahead, Chapter 7 will be our final chapter and will introduce the remaining 'ending' letters: ף (Pe Sofit), ך (Kaf Sofit), and ץ (Tsadi Sofit). These special forms are crucial for mastering proper

Hebrew writing and pronunciation. In addition, we will delve into the guttural letters ח (Chet) and ע (Ayin).

Chapter 7– Gutturals and Other Endings

Thinking about ideas was born hand in hand with language.

חֲשִׁיבָה עַל רַעְיוֹנוֹת נוֹלְדָה יָד בְּיָד עִם שָׂפָה.

Konrad Lorenz קוֹנְרָד לוֹרֶנְץ -

Almost there! Welcome to the final chapter of this book. We will explore some remaining aspects of pronunciation: the guttural letters and the remaining final forms of letters.

We will begin by focusing on the guttural letters Chet (ח), and Ayin (ע), but will try to understand them in the larger context of guttural and non-guttural sounds in Hebrew. These letters are produced using the back part of the vocal tract. Understanding guttural letters is essential for capturing the authentic sound of Hebrew and for mastering more advanced aspects of the language. It is also the most difficult aspect for those who speak English or Spanish.

Another key focus of this chapter is the final forms of certain letters, known in Hebrew as 'Sofit' letters. These special forms – Tsade Sofit (ץ), Pe Sofit (ף), and Kaf Sofit (ך) – appear only at the end of words and have unique pronunciations and writing styles.

By the end of this chapter, you will have a more comprehensive grasp of Hebrew phonetics, enabling you to read, write, and speak with greater accuracy and confidence.

Name of Letter	Transliterated	Sound	Consonants
alef	---	.	א
vet	v	[v]	ב
bet	b	[b]	בּ

Name of Vowel	Transliterated	Sound	Nikud
shva nach		STOP	ט
chataf patach	a	ah	ח
chataf kamatz			ח

gimel	g	[g]	ג
dalet	d	[d]	ד
he	h	[h]	ה
vav	v	[v]	ו
zayin	z	[z]	ז
chet	ch	[χ]	ח
tet	t	[t]	ט
yod	y	[y]	י
khaf, **khaf sofit**	kh	[c]	כ ך
kaf	c, k	[k]	כּ
lamed	l	[l]	ל
mem, mem sofit	m	[m]	מ ם
nun, nun sofit	n	[n]	נ ן
samech	s	[s]	ס
ayin	---	-	ע

patach			טַ
kamatz			טָ
tzeire			טֵ
segol	e	eh	טֶ
chataf segol			חֱ
chirik	i	ee	טִ
chirik male			טִי
cholam	o	oh	טֹ
cholam male			טוֹ
kubutz	u	oo	טֻ
shuruk			טוּ

fei, **fei sofit**	f	[f]	פ ף
pei	p	[p]	פ
tzadi, **tzadi sofit**	tz, ts	[ts]	צ ץ
kuf	c, k	[k]	ק
reish	r, rr	[r]	ר
shin	sh	[sh]	שׁ
sin	s	[s]	שׂ
tav	t	[t]	ת

Shva Sounds

The Shva (שְׁוָא) is a Hebrew vowel sign represented by two vertical dots under a letter. It has two main forms: the simple Shva and Chataf vowels.

1. **Simple Shva (שְׁוָא נָח):**

   - Can be either silent (Shva Nach) or pronounced as a very quick 'eh' (Shva Na).

   - When silent, it typically appears at the beginning of a word or under a letter without a preceding vowel.

   - When pronounced, it generally follows a vowel and creates a slight 'eh' sound, as in the Hebrew for "in" (בְּ).

2. **Chataf Vowels:**

- These are a combination of Shva with one of three short vowels: Patach, Segol, or Kamatz.

- **Chataf Patach (חֲ):** Combines a short 'a' sound with Shva, pronounced as 'ah', as in חֲמִי (mercy).

- **Chataf Segol (חֱ):** Combines a short 'e' sound with Shva, pronounced as 'eh', as in בֶּטֶן (stomach).

- **Chataf Kamatz (חֳ):** Combines a short 'o' sound with Shva, pronounced as 'oh', as in חֳלָם (dream).

Guttural Letters

Guttural letters in Hebrew are a group of consonants pronounced using the back part of the vocal tract. They are distinct in their sound and often influence the vowels that accompany them. The primary guttural letters in Hebrew are:

1. **Aleph (א):** Though often silent, it acts as a carrier for vowels and is considered a guttural letter.

2. **He (ה):** Has a light, breathy sound, much like the 'h' in "hat."

3. **Chet (ח):** A pronounced, guttural sound similar to the Scottish 'loch' or the German 'Bach.'

4. **Ayin (ע):** Historically a deep, guttural sound, though in modern Hebrew, it's often silent or very lightly pronounced.

Guttural letters can affect the pronunciation of nearby vowels and often have special rules in grammar, particularly in verbs and nouns.

- Guttural sounds in Hebrew are produced from the back of the throat or the back of the mouth.
- These sounds are typically deeper and more resonant compared to other Hebrew sounds.

- Guttural letters in Hebrew, including Chet, Ayin, and Resh, are often considered a separate class due to their distinct phonetic qualities.
- They play a unique role in Hebrew pronunciation and carry special significance in terms of their spiritual and symbolic meanings in Jewish tradition.

Het

Het (ח), sometimes spelled Chet, is a guttural letter in the Hebrew alphabet. It is pronounced with a deep throat sound, similar to the 'ch' in the Scottish word "loch" or the German "Bach." It is distinctly harsher and deeper than Kaf (כ), which is more front-of-the-mouth and lighter.

To write Het in block style:

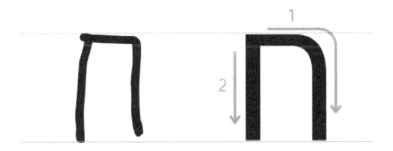

Practice: Write several iterations of *Het* below.

			ח	ח	ח
_____	_____	_____	_____	_____	_____
_____	_____	_____	_____	_____	_____

Practice: Below is a combined list of Hebrew letters and vowels, with an emphasis on **Het**. Try to pronounce the written letters on the right *without* using the transliteration on the left.

Pronunciation	Hebrew Word
'chai'	חַי
'lay-chah'	לֵיחָה
'chor'	חוֹר
'me-chit'	מְחִית
'chadsh'	חַדְשׁ
'chak'	חָק
'ree-ach'	רֵיחַ
'chal-mon'	חַלְמוֹן
'chokh-mah'	חָכְמָה
'cheel'	חִיל

Ayin

Ayin (ע) is a unique letter in the Hebrew alphabet. Historically, it represents a deep, guttural sound not found in English, but in modern Hebrew, it is often pronounced as a glottal stop or is silent. Ayin represents the number seventy in the Hebrew alphabet and numerology. The word Ayin means "eye," symbolizing perception, insight, and knowledge. The letter was written in the shape of an eye in ancient Hebrew. While Aleph is often silent or a soft glottal stop, Ayin has a more noticeable and pronounced guttural sound.

To write Ayin in block style:

Practice: Write several iterations of *Ayin* below.

____	____		ע	ע	**ע**
____	____	____	____	____	____

Practice: Below is a combined list of Hebrew letters and vowels, with an emphasis on **Ayin**. Try to pronounce the written letters on the right *without* using the transliteration on the left.

Pronunciation	**Hebrew Word**
'az'	עַז
'ma-ah-leh'	מַעֲלֶה
'or'	עוֹר
'eer'	עִיר
'ad'	עַד

Pronunciation	Hebrew Word
'erev'	עֶרֶב
'ro-eh'	רֹעֶה
'a-lum'	עָלוּם
'a-nan'	עָנָן
'ee-ton'	עִיתוֹן

Final Letters (Endings)

Additional and final letters - these letters are always Soft!

Tsade sofit

The name Tzadi may have originated from a fast recitation of the alphabet, influenced by the Hebrew word tzadik, meaning "righteous person." The exact origin of ṣade, which the letter Tzadi represents, is unclear. Picture Tzadi Sofit as a righteous person standing firm and tall at the end of a word. This image can help you remember its unique final form and its association with the concept of righteousness.

To write Tsade Sofit in block style:

Practice: Write several iterations of *Tsadi Sofit* below.

——	——		Y	Y	Y
——	——	——	——	——	——

Pe Sofit

Pe Sofit is the final form of the letter Pe, which is assumed to have originated from a pictogram of a "mouth" (in Hebrew, pe). This letter is one of the six that can receive a Dagesh Kal, which can affect its pronunciation. Imagine Pe Sofit as an artistic representation of a mouth that's slightly open at the end of a word, as if it's finishing a statement. This can help recall its appearance and its special use at the end of words.

To write Pe Sofit in block style:

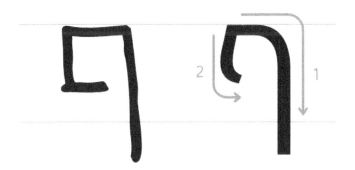

Practice: Write several iterations of *Pe Sofit* below.

			ף	ף	ף

Khaf Sofit

Kaf Sofit is one of the five Hebrew letters with a final form. This form changes when the letter appears at the end of a word. The letter Kaf Sofit is pronounced as a Khaf in this position. These letters originally served a punctuation purpose, indicating the end of a sentence or a pause. Visualize Kaf Sofit as a hand (kaf) waving goodbye at the end of a word. This imagery aligns with its appearance only at the end of words and its pronunciation.

To write Khaf Sofit in block style:

Practice: Write several iterations of *Khaf Sofit* below.

			ך	ך	ך

Chapter Summary

→ **Deep Dive into Guttural Letters**: We focused on the guttural letters in Hebrew, including Aleph (א), He (ה), Chet (ח), and Ayin (ע). These letters are characterized by their distinct sounds produced in the back of the vocal tract. They have a special role in Hebrew pronunciation.

→ **Final Letters**: The chapter also covered the final forms of certain Hebrew letters, specifically Tsade Sofit (ץ), Pe Sofit (ף), and Kaf Sofit (ך). These final forms are used exclusively at the end of words.

Practice

Exercise 1:

Use the transliterations in the middle column as a guide to write the corresponding Hebrew words in the right column. Focus particularly on practicing the Hebrew letters of this chapter: ח, ע, ף, ך, and ץ. This exercise is designed to help you familiarize yourself with the shapes and forms of these specific letters in their written form.

#	Transliteration	Hebrew
1	larutz	_____
2	ketzef	_____
3	ruach	_____
4	roch	_____
5	lehadof	_____
6	yam suf	_____
7	meshkaf	_____
8	hafuch	_____
9	koretz	_____
10	korech	_____
11	roa	_____

12	tzuk	_____
13	cham velach	_____
14	yehonatan	_____
15	hedef	_____
16	berkovitz	_____
17	memshala	_____
18	karua	_____
19	tzatz	_____
20	atzitz	_____

Exercise 2:

For each transliteration in the middle column, choose the correctly spelled word from the two options provided in the right column, each with Nikud. This exercise will help you practice distinguishing between similar-looking Hebrew words and understanding the importance of correct spelling and Nikud in the Hebrew language.

	Transliteration	Choices
1	Yodea	יוֹדֵעַ או יוֹדֵא
2	Kore	קוֹרֵא או קוֹרֵעַ

3	Haskala	הַשְׂכָּלָה או אַשְׂכָּלָה
4	Moach	מֹחַ או מוֹךְ
5	Choshev	חוֹשֵׁב או כּוֹשֵׁב
6	Mad'an	מַדְעָן או מַדָּן
7	Lechem	לֶחֶם או לַכֶם
8	Mevade	מֻדָּא או מוֹוָדַע
9	Gavoah	גְּבוֹהַ או גָּבוֹחַ
10	Ozen	אוֹזֶן או הוֹזֶן
11	Ma'amul	מַעֲמוּל או מַאֲמוּל
12	Kafe	קָפֶה או קָפֵע
13	Stav	סְתָיו או סְתָב

Exercise 3:

Look at the Hebrew words in the right column, each with Nikud, and write their transliteration in the corresponding blank space in the middle column. This exercise will help you practice converting Hebrew words into their phonetic English equivalents, focusing on the correct pronunciation, and understanding of each word.

Transliteration	**Hebrew Word**

_____	חַלּוֹן	1
_____	עוֹלָם	2
_____	בָּרוּךְ	3
_____	עֵץ	4
_____	מַחְשֵׁב	5
_____	עִיר	6
_____	לֵילָךְ	7
_____	חוֹל	8
_____	עֲנָנִים	9
_____	חַג	10
_____	עָפִיף	11
_____	רֵיחַ	12
_____	עֶרֶב	13
_____	חַי	14
_____	עַד	15

חֲנוּכָּה **16** _____

עֶגְלָה **17** _____

עֶקָר **18** _____

חָלָב **19**

_____   חֲנוּכָּה **16**

_____   עֶגְלָה **17**

_____   עֶקָר **18**

חָלָב **19**

Chapter 7 Answer Key

Exercise 1:

No.	Answer
1	לרוץ
2	קצף
3	רוח
4	רוך
5	להדוף
6	ים סוף
7	משקף
8	הפוך
9	קורץ
10	כורך
11	רוע
12	צוק

13	חם ולח
14	יהונתן
15	הדף
16	ברקוביץ
17	ממשלה
18	קרוע
19	צץ
20	עציץ

Exercise 2:

No.	Answer
1	יודע
2	קורע
3	השכלה
4	מוח

5	חושב
6	מדען
7	לחם
8	מוודא
9	גבוה
10	אוזן
11	מעמול
12	קפה
13	סתיו

Exercise 3:

No.	Answer
1	khalon
2	olam
3	barukh
4	etz

5	makh'shev
6	ir
7	leilakh
8	khol
9	ananim
10	chag
11	afif
12	reyach
13	erev
14	chai
15	ed
16	khanuka
17	agala
18	akar
19	chalav

Conclusion

The higher the culture, the richer the language.

כָּל שֶׁהַתַּרְבּוּת גְּבוֹהָה יוֹתֵר, כָּךְ הַשָּׂפָה עֲשִׁירָה יוֹתֵר.

- Anton Chekhov אַנְטוֹן צֶ'כוֹב

Hebrew, with its ancient roots and modern vibrancy, serves not just as a means of communication, but as a gateway to a deep and storied culture.

In this book, we've travelled from the very basics of the Alef-Bet to the complexities of guttural letters and final forms. You've learned about the peculiarities of Hebrew phonetics. The skills you've acquired here lay the groundwork for further exploration and mastery. The upcoming books in this series, focusing on grammar and vocabulary, will build upon this foundation. They will transform your basic understanding into a comprehensive grasp of the language. Using your knowledge of the alef-bet, you will be able to not only engage with Hebrew texts, but also converse fluently, and immerse yourself fully in Hebrew-speaking environments.

The second book will delve into the intricate world of Hebrew grammar - a simple yet essential system to learn in order to be able to construct actual sentences. This will include verb conjugations, noun-adjective agreements, and the usage of prepositions and conjunctions. Through this, you will start to see how the building blocks of Hebrew come together in a coherent and logical manner.

The third book will expand your vocabulary and speaking skills and introduce you to a wide array of words and phrases, all based on your knowledge of grammar acquired from the second book. This will not only enhance your speaking and reading skills but also deepen your understanding of Israeli culture and Jewish history. With each new word, you'll gain insights into the values, traditions, and experiences that have shaped the Hebrew language over centuries.

Congratulations on completing this book. Best wishes as you continue your language journey with the next steps in the series!

BOOK 2

Complete Hebrew Workbook for Adult Beginners: *Writing*

Write Hebrew In 30 Days!

Explore to Win

Introduction

מָבוֹא

(MaVo)

To understand the structure of a language is to understand its soul.

להבין את מבנה שפה הוא להבין את נשמתה

Welcome to Book 2 of the "Learn Hebrew for Adult Beginners: 3 Books in 1" series. You nailed Book 1 and have the Alef-Bet under your belt – congratulations! Now, we're going to turn you into a Hebrew Krav-Maga expert (Israeli martial arts) with some in-depth *dikduk* - דקדוק - grammar! Hebrew, a language of ancient origins, presents a unique and intriguing challenge for learners. Its structure and composition are not just about memorizing rules and vocabulary but also understanding its inherent logic.

For example, Hebrew verb structures are called 'binyanim.' There are seven binyanim in Hebrew, each serving a unique function in the language. These verb structures are basically templates into which roots are placed to form verbs, with each binyan altering the root to convey different nuances of action or state.

So then, what are roots? Normally, they are three Hebrew letters that are plugged into different verb and noun structures to convey similar meanings. Trust me, learning all about roots is *key* to unlocking your Hebrew skills faster and more effectively.

And, in terms of expressing time, Hebrew simplifies this aspect with just three tenses: past, present, and future. This streamlined approach contrasts with more complex tense systems found in other languages, like English. Each tense in Hebrew has its own unique conjugation pattern, integral to accurately expressing time-related concepts.

By the end of this book, you won't just understand Hebrew, you'll get how it *thinks*. We'll use the same method as in Book 1: clear explanations, tons of examples, and exercises to burn it into your brain.

This isn't some boring textbook; learning Hebrew is a trip! Soon, you'll be slinging Hebrew without even thinking about it.

Remember our 30-day Hebrew goal. Every bit of grammar you learn brings you closer to fluency. It is in no way easy, but the payoff for learning a number of universal rules is huge.

~

Embrace the challenge today.

Experience the joy of speaking Hebrew in just 30 days.

Chapter 1 – Basic Grammar

Every language is a new world.

כָּל שָׂפָה הִיא עוֹלָם חָדָשׁ

In Hebrew, adjectives typically follow the nouns they modify. For instance, "tall woman" in Hebrew would be expressed as "woman tall."

Hebrew grammar also presents a uniquely "invisible is." See, unlike English, the present tense of the verb "to be" (is, are) is often implied rather than explicitly stated. This might seem unusual at first, but it becomes second nature with practice.

Let's explore this concept through colors! Here's a table of the common Hebrew colors and their English translations: Now, let's see the "invisible is" in action with some examples:

English	(Transliteration)	Hebrew
Red	Adom	אדום
Blue	Kachol	כחול
Green	Yarok	ירוק
Yellow	Tzahov	צהוב
Black	Shachor	שחור

White	Lavan	לבן
Purple	Sagol	סגול
Orange	Katom	כתום
Pink	Varod	ורוד
Brown	Chum	חום

Now, notice how there's no "is" or "are" in the following Hebrew sentences:

- אדום האוטובוס - The bus is red
- כחולים השמיים - The sky is blue
- ירוקים העלים - The leaves are green

Now, let's see how these colors are used in more sentences with the "invisible is." Below is a table with Hebrew sentences, their transliteration, a literal translation, and the implied English translation:

Actual Translation	"Literal" Meaning	Transliteration	Hebrew Sentence
The table is green	The table green	HaShulchan Yarok	השולחן ירוק
The apple is red	The apple red	HaTapuach Adom	התפוח אדום

The sky is blue	The sky blue	HaShamayim K'cholim	השמים כחול
The shirt is yellow	The shirt yellow	HaChultza Tzahovah	החולצה צהובה
The cat is black	The cat black	HaChatul Shachor	החתול שחור
The cloud is white	The cloud white	HaAnan Lavan	הענן לבן
The flower is purple	The flower purple	HaPerach Sagol	הפרח סגול
The car is orange	The car orange	HaRechev Katom	הרכב כתום
The balloon is pink	The balloon pink	HaBalon Varod	הבלון ורוד
The door is brown	The door brown	HaDelet Chuma	הדלת חומה

Notice how the Hebrew sentences lack a direct equivalent of "is" or "are." This gives Hebrew a specific flow. As you learn, you'll instinctively know when the "invisible is" applies.

Definite Articles with Nouns and Adjectives

The letter *he* (ה) also acts as the definite article in Hebrew, much like the word "the" in English. By prefixing *He* to a noun, it shifts from being indefinite to definite. There is no method of "a" or "an" in Hebrew; it's only undefined and defined as with *He*.

Note: There are other methods of defining nouns in Hebrew (without using ה), but these are more uncommon and will be touched on in Book III.

Practice: Below is a list of Hebrew nouns from before; some are defined by "the", while others are undefined without "the". Try to determine which is which. You can check your answers in the left column.

Transliteration	Hebrew Word
halayil *(the night)*	הַלַּיִל
rut *(Ruth)*	רוּת
daveed *(David)*	דָּוִד
hatorah *(the Torah)*	הַתּוֹרָה
dor *(a generation)*	דּוֹר
hayadid *(the friend)*	הַיָּדִיד
golah *(an exile)*	גּוֹלָה
hatahor *(the pure)*	הַטָּהוֹר
hamoreh *(the teacher)*	הַמּוֹרֶה
sirah *(a boat)*	סִירָה
kool *("cool")*	קוּל
hazikah *(a passion)*	הַזִּיקָה
hara'ui *(the worthy)*	הָרָאוּי
toda *("thank you")*	תּוֹדָה

הַנּוֹצָה

When both a noun and its modifying adjective have the definite article "ה" (Ha), it indicates that the adjective is describing a specific, definite noun. This is akin to saying "the [adjective] [noun]" in English.

Translation	Transliteration	Hebrew Sentence
The red table	HaShulchan HaAdom	השולחן האדום
The green apple	HaTapuach HaYarok	התפוח הירוק
The blue sky	HaShamayim HaKchulim	השמים הכחולים
The yellow shirt	HaChultza HaTzahovah	החולצה הצהובה
The black cat	HaChatul HaShachor	החתול השחור

In each of the above sentences, both the noun and the adjective are preceded by "ה" (He), signifying that we are talking about a **specific** object (e.g., "the red table", not just *any* red table).

Sentences without Definite Articles

When neither the noun nor the adjective has the definite article "ה" (Ha), it refers to a non-specific or indefinite item, similar to using "a" or "an" in English.

Let's see how this works in practice:

Translation	Transliteration	Hebrew Sentence

A red table	Shulchan Adom	שולחן אדום
A green apple	Tapuach Yarok	תפוח ירוק
Blue skies	Shamayim Kacholim	שמים כחולים
A yellow shirt	Chultza Tzahovah	חולצה צהובה
A black cat	Chatul Shachor	חתול שחור

The following is a table with some common descriptive adjectives about appearance, their transliterations, and English translations:

English Translation	Hebrew (Transliteration)	Hebrew (Written)
Beautiful	Yafeh	יָפֶה
Ugly	Mekho'ar	מְכוֹעָר
Strong	Chazak	חָזָק
Weak	Chalash	חַלָּשׁ
Far	Rachok	רָחוֹק
Near/Close	Karov	קָרוֹב

Tall	Gavoha	גָבוֹהַ
Short	Namuch	נָמוּךְ
Small	Katan	קָטָן
Big/Large	Gadol	גָדוֹל
Pale	Chiver	חיוור
Tanned	Shazuf	שָׁזוּף

Chapter 1 Summary

This chapter established the essential foundations for beginning your Hebrew learning journey:

→ **Grammar**: Introduced the basic structure of Hebrew sentences, focusing on the use of definite articles ('ה') and their role in making nouns and adjectives definite.

→ **Adjectives:** Explained the placement of adjectives in Hebrew, which typically follow the nouns they modify. Emphasized the agreement of adjectives with the definiteness of nouns.

→ **Is**: Discussed the concept of the "invisible is" in Hebrew, where the verb "to be" is often implied in present-tense sentences but not explicitly stated.

→ **Colors**: Introduced common color adjectives in Hebrew, providing examples of how they are used in sentences with and without definite articles.

→ **Descriptive Words (Appearance)**: Presented basic adjectives for describing appearance, such as 'גבוה' (tall), 'קטן' (small), and their application in sentence construction.

Practice

Exercise 1:

In each sentence, decide whether the noun and adjective should be definite or indefinite in Hebrew based on the English phrase given. Fill in each blank with 'ה' if the word is definite, if it is a descriptive sentence, or leave the definite article out if it is not needed.

No.	English Phrase	Hebrew Phrase
1	The red flower	_פרח _אדום
2	A small table	_שולחן _קטן
3	The table is small	_שולחן _קטן
4	A blue sky	_שמים _כחולים
5	The green apple	_תפוח _ירוק
6	A tall tree	_עץ _גבוה
7	The shirt is yellow	_חולצה _צהובה
8	The black cat	_חתול _שחור
9	A white cloud	_ענן _לבן
10	The big table	_שולחן _גדול

Exercise 2:

Below are several Hebrew phrases featuring a mix of nouns and adjectives. Determine what each phrase means. The phrases could translate to either "the [adjective] [noun]", "a [adjective] [noun]", or "the [noun] is [adjective]".

No.	Possible Meanings	Hebrew
1	a) The small dog b) A small dog c) The dog is small	הכלב הקטן
2	a) The tall tree b) A tall tree c) The tree is tall	עץ גבוה
3	a) The yellow flower b) A yellow flower c) The flower is yellow	הפרח צהוב
4	a) The red apple b) A red apple c) The apple is red	תפוח אדום
5	a) The blue sky b) A blue sky c) The sky is blue	השמים כחולים
6	a) The black cat b) A black cat c) The cat is black	חתול שחור
7	a) The big table b) A big table c) The table is big	השולחן גדול
8	a) The small table b) A small table c) The table is small	שולחן קטן
9	a) The green tree b) A green tree c) The tree is green	העץ ירוק
10	a) The yellow shirt b) A yellow shirt c) The shirt is yellow	חולצה צהובה

Exercise 3:

Use the following word bank of nouns and adjectives to create Hebrew phrases based on the English prompts. Remember to apply the correct use of definite articles and the concept of the 'invisible is'. All words are masculine.

Word Bank:

- Nouns: חתול (cat), שולחן (table), כלב (dog), עץ (tree), פרח (flower)

- Adjectives: שחור (black), קטן (small), גבוה (tall), צהוב (yellow), אדום (red)

No.	English Prompt	Your Hebrew Phrase
1	The black cat	
2	A small table	
3	The dog is small	
4	A tall tree	
5	The flower is yellow	
6	The red flower	
7	A yellow dog	
8	The table is small	
9	The tree is tall	
10	A black cat	

Chapter 1 Answer Key

Exercise 1:

No.	Answer
1	הפרח האדום
2	שולחן קטן
3	השולחן קטן
4	שמים כחולים
5	התפוח הירוק
6	עץ גבוה
7	החולצה צהובה
8	החתול השחור
9	ענן לבן
10	השולחן הגדול

Exercise 2:

No.	Answer
1	c) The dog is small
2	b) A tall tree
3	c) The flower is yellow
4	b) A red apple
5	c) The sky is blue
6	b) A black cat
7	c) The table is big
8	b) A small table
9	c) The tree is green
10	a) The yellow shirt

Exercise 3:

No.	Hebrew Phrase
1	החתול השחור
2	שולחן קטן
3	הכלב קטן

Coming up...

In the next chapter, Chapter 2, we delve deeper into gender (male and female nouns and adjectives), plurality (including how it affects adjectives), and introduce the use of pronouns.

Chapter 2 – Gender and Plurality

To learn a language is to have one more window from which to look at the world.

לִלְמוֹד שָׂפָה זֶה לִפְתּוֹחַ עוֹד חַלּוֹן לְהַשְׁקִיף מִמֶּנּוּ עַל הָעוֹלָם

Remember how adjectives always followed the nouns they described? Well, Hebrew nouns (and the adjectives describing them) also have genders: masculine or feminine. Don't worry, there are patterns to learn that make this less tricky than it sounds!

In this chapter, we will cover genders and plurals – how to change a word to talk about many things instead of just one. Finally, we'll introduce pronouns, including modifiers like "this", "that", and "these". In Hebrew, pronouns also change depending on gender and number, which allows for very specific descriptions (in complex sentences, for example).

Male and Female

All nouns have a gender. Knowing a word's gender is key, because it affects everything from the adjectives describing that word to the verbs you use with it. It's also a fairly straightforward process.

A helpful rule is that many feminine nouns and adjectives end in the letter ת (Tav) or ה (He). Here are some examples:

- **Nouns with ת (Tav):**

    ○ מכונית Car - *Mechonit*

    ○ רקדנית Female dancer - *Rakdanit*

    ○ מברשת Brush - *Mivreshet*

- **Nouns with ה (He):**

- ○ משפחה Family - *Mishpacha*

- ○ מילה Word - *Mila*

- ○ שמלה Dress - *Simla*

- ○ מורה Female teacher - *Mora*

Important Note: Not *every* word ending in these letters is feminine, but it's a common pattern that helps you get started! For example:

- ○ שמש Sun - *Shemesh*

Hebrew names are another great way to see gender in action:

- דן Male name - *Dan*

- דנה Female name (note the added *he*) - *Dana*

- מיכל Female name - *Mikhal*

Adjectives Following Gender

Adjectives in Hebrew must agree in gender with the noun they modify. This means that if a noun is feminine, the adjective describing it must also be in its feminine form. For example:

- השולחן גדול (HaShulchan Gadol) – The table is big (masculine).
- הספה גדולה (HaSapa Gedolah) – The sofa is big (feminine).

Plural

Plurality in Hebrew, like in many languages, involves modifying a word to indicate more than one of something. In Hebrew, this often means adding specific suffixes to nouns and adjectives. The two primary suffixes for plural forms are ים (Yim) for masculine words and ות (Ot) for feminine words. While there are exceptions, these suffixes are reliable indicators of gender in plural forms.

Masculine Plural: ים (Yim)

Masculine nouns and adjectives typically adopt the ים (Yim) suffix in their plural forms. For example:

- כלב – Dog - *Kelev*
- כלבים – Dogs - *Klavim*

Feminine Plural: ות (Ot)

Feminine nouns and adjectives typically use the ות (Ot) suffix in their plural forms:

- חתולה - Cat - *Chatula*
- חתולות - Cats - *Chatulot*

Let's introduce some family member nouns to practice these plural forms:

- אח - Brother - *Ach*
- אחים - Brothers - *Achim*
- אמא - Mother - *Ima*
- אמהות - Mothers - *Imahot*

Using these words in phrases:

- האח הגדול - The big brother
- האחים הגדולים - The big brothers
- האמא היפה - The beautiful mother
- האמהות היפות - The beautiful mothers

While ים (Yim) and ות (Ot) are commonly used for masculine and feminine plurals, respectively, Hebrew has its exceptions. Some words might not follow this pattern, and their plural forms need to be memorized separately. However, in most cases, these suffixes are reliable indicators. For example:

- שולחן - Table (male) - *Shulchan*

- שולחנות - Tables (male plural) - *Shulchanot*

Our Hebrew Family Tree

Let's expand your Hebrew vocabulary with words for those closest to you – your family! Here's a table of common family terms, along with their pronunciations and notes on gender:

Notes	English Translation	Hebrew (Transliteration)	Hebrew (Written)
Masculine	Dad/Father	Aba	אבא
Feminine	Mom/Mother	Ima	אימא
Masculine	Brother	Ach	אח
Feminine	Sister	Achot	אחות
Masculine	Grandfather	Saba	סבא
Feminine	Grandmother	Savta	סבתא
Masculine	Uncle (father's or mother's brother)	Dod	דוד

Feminine	Aunt (father's or mother's sister)	Doda	דודה
Masculine	Son	Ben	בן
Feminine	Daughter	Bat	בת

- You can add the word "קטן" (katan - small) or "קטנה" (ktana - small, feminine) to describe younger siblings - e.g., אחות קטנה (achot ktana) for "little sister."
- For older siblings, use "גדול" (gadol - big, masculine) or "גדולה" (gdola - big, feminine) – e.g., אח גדול (ach gadol) for "big brother."

Pronouns

Pronouns like "this," "they," and "I" are essential for describing and making connections in any language. Here's your guide to the core Hebrew pronouns:

Notes	Gender	Transliteration	Hebrew	English
Used by everyone	Masculine or Feminine	Ani	אני	I
-	Masculine	Ata	אתה	You (masculine, singular)
-	Feminine	At	את	You (feminine, singular)
-	Masculine	Hu	הוא	He
-	Feminine	Hi	היא	She

Used by everyone	Masculine or Feminine	Anachnu	אנחנו	We
Important choice – match speaker's group!	Masculine / Feminine	Atem (m) / Aten (f)	אתם / אתן	You (plural)
-	Masculine	Hem	הם	They (masculine)
-	Feminine	Hen	הן	They (feminine)
-	Masculine	Ze	זה	This (masculine)
-	Feminine	Zot	זאת	This (feminine)
Refers to both masculine & feminine things	Masculine or Feminine	Ele	אלה	These
A bit like "that one over there"	Masculine	Ha'hu	ההוא	That (masculine)
A bit like "that one over there"	Feminine	Ha'hi	ההיא	That (feminine)
-	Masculine	Ha'hem	ההם	Those (masculine)
-	Feminine	Ha'hen	ההן	Those (feminine)

- Speaking about a father: "אבא שלי הוא גבוה" (My father, he is tall).

- Referring to a sister: "אחותי היא חכמה" (My sister, she is smart).

- Talking about cousins: "בני הדוד שלי הם צעירים" (My male cousins, they are young) or

  "בנות הדודה שלי הן ספורטאיות" (My female cousins, they are athletes).

Basic Rules for Definite Articles with Pronouns

1. When a pronoun and noun are used without the definite article 'ה' (Ha), it generally refers to an indefinite subject.

   - "הוא אח" - He is a brother

2. Adding the definite article to the pronoun but not the noun specifies a particular subject but keeps the noun general.

   - "הוא האח" - He is THE brother

3. When both the pronoun and noun have the definite article, it refers to a specific subject and a specific object.

   - "האח ההוא" - THAT brother

   - "היא אחות" - She is a sister

   - "היא האחות" - She is THE sister

   - "האחות ההיא" - THAT sister

Chapter 2 Summary

This chapter established the essential foundations for beginning your Hebrew learning journey:

➜ **Male and Female**: Introduced the concept of gender in Hebrew grammar. Focused on how nouns and adjectives change based on masculine and feminine forms, often indicated by specific endings like ת (Tav) and ה (He).

➜ **Plural:** Explored the use of plural forms in Hebrew, primarily using the suffixes םי (Yim) for masculine words and תו (Ot) for feminine words.

➜ **Pronouns**: Discussed various Hebrew pronouns, including those for 'this', 'that', 'these', 'those', and how they align with the gender and number of the nouns they refer to or replace.

➜ **Family**: Introduced common Hebrew words for family members.

Practice

Exercise 1:

In these exercises, you will modify Hebrew nouns and adjectives by adding the correct definite articles and plural suffixes. To help you choose the correct gender-based endings, each Hebrew noun is marked with either (ז) for זכר (Zachar, masculine) or (נ) for נקבה (Nekevah, feminine).

No.	English Phrase	Hebrew Phrase (Basic Form)
1	The red flowers	(פרח) (אדום)
2	A small table	(שולחן) (קטן)
3	The big tables	שולחן גדול
4	A blue sky	שמים כחולים
5	The green apples	תפוח ירוק
6	A tall tree	עץ גבוה
7	The yellow shirts	חולצה צהובה
8	The black cats	חתול שחור
9	A white cloud	ענן לבן
10	The small dogs	כלב קטן

11	The brothers	אח
12	A sister	אחות
13	The tall brothers	אח גבוה
14	The white houses	בית לבן
15	A black computer	מחשב שחור

Exercise 2:

Fill in the blank with the appropriate Hebrew pronoun. Use the prompts in parentheses to guide your choice.

No.		Phrase with Blank
1		(I) ____ גבוה (ו
2		האחים (those) ____ גדולים
3		(She) ____ יפה
4		(We) ____ בבית
5		התפוחים (these) ____ טעימים
6		(You, fem.) ____ אוכלת

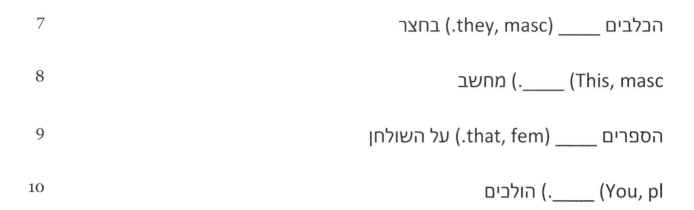

7	הכלבים ____ (they, masc.) בחצר
8	____ (This, masc.) מחשב.
9	הספרים ____ (that, fem.) על השולחן.
10	הולכים ____ (You, pl.)

Exercise 3:

Use the word bank provided to construct the correct Hebrew phrase based on the English sentence. Pay attention to gender, plurality, definite articles, and pronoun usage as discussed in our previous conversations.

Word Bank

- חתול(Cat)
- שחור(Black)
- גדול(Big)
- אחים(Brothers)
- תפוחים(Apples)
- ירוקים(Green)
- זה(This - masc.)
- זאת(This - fem.)
- הם(They - masc.)
- הן(They - fem.)

- שולחנות (Tables)

- קטנים (Small)

Fill in the blanks with the appropriate words from the word bank to correctly translate the English sentences into Hebrew.

No.	English Sentence	Hebrew Sentence (Fill in the blanks)
1	This is a black cat.	_____ _____ _____
2	Those are big tables.	_____ _____ _____
3	These are green apples.	_____ _____ _____
4	She is a sister.	_____ _____
5	The brothers are tall.	_____ _____ _____
6	This is a small apple.	_____ _____ _____
7	The dogs are black.	_____ _____ _____
8	Those tables are small.	_____ _____ _____
9	The cat is big.	_____ _____ _____
10	These apples are green.	_____ _____ _____

Chapter 2 Answer Key

Exercise 1:

No.	Correct Hebrew Phrase
1	הפרחים האדומים
2	שולחן קטן
3	השולחנות הגדולים
4	שמים כחולים
5	התפוחים הירוקים
6	עץ גבוה
7	החולצות הצהובות
8	החתולים השחורים
9	ענן לבן
10	הכלבים הקטנים
11	האחים
12	אחות

13	האחים הגבוהים
14	הבתים הלבנים
15	מחשב שחור

Exercise 2:

No.	Correct Phrase
1	אני גבוה
2	האחים ההם גדולים
3	היא יפה
4	אנחנו בבית
5	התפוחים אלה טעימים
6	את אוכלת
7	הכלבים הם בחצר
8	זה מחשב
9	הספרים ההן על השולחן
10	אתם הולכים

No.	Correct Hebrew Sentence
1	זה חתול שחור
2	הם שולחנות גדולים
3	אלה תפוחים ירוקים
4	היא אחות
5	האחים גבוהים
6	זה תפוח קטן
7	הכלבים שחורים
8	השולחנות ההם קטנים
9	החתול גדול
10	התפוחים האלה ירוקים

Coming up...

In the next chapter, Chapter 3, we will begin to explore Hebrew verbs and prepositions. We will delve into the different verb tenses, focusing on their formation and usage in various contexts.

Chapter 3 – Verbs and Prepositions

Language is the roadmap of a culture.

הַשָּׂפָה הִיא מַפַּת הַדֶּרֶךְ שֶׁל הַתַּרְבּוּת

Hebrew verbs are categorized into seven main structures, or "buildings," known as בניינים (Binyanim). Each בניין (Binyan) follows a unique pattern that dictates how verbs are conjugated across different tenses. The seven בניינים are:

1. פעל (Pa'al)
2. נפעל (Nif'al)
3. פיעל (Pi'el)
4. הפעיל (Hif'il)
5. התפעל (Hitpa'el)
6. פועל (Po'al)
7. הופעל (Huf'al)

These structures are consistent in their pattern for each tense, providing a reliable framework for verb conjugation. The name of each בניין is derived from the "he" form of the past tense of that verb structure (e.g., בניין פעל for פעל הוא). More on this later.

The present tense in בניין פעל typically has four main forms, which can be represented generically as follows:

1. **Masculine Singular**: פועל (Po'el)

2. **Feminine Singular**: פועלת (Po'elet)

3. **Masculine Plural**: פועלים (Po'alim)

4. **Feminine Plural**: פועלות (Po'alot)

Infinitives

Infinitives are powerful tools that let you express actions, states, or processes as nouns. They're foundational to Hebrew grammar and essential for mastering the language.

The five main binyanim (פעל, פיעל, הפעיל, נפעל, התפעל) are verb patterns that change the meaning and form of the root verb. Each binyan has its own infinitive form:

Example	Infinitive Prefix	Binyan
לִכְתּוֹב - To write	לִפְעֹל (li-f'ol)	פעל
לְלַמֵּד - To teach	לְפַעֵל (le-fa'el)	פיעל
לְהַבְרִיא - To recover (from illness)	לְהַפְעִיל (le-haf'il)	הפעיל
לְהִפָּגֵש - To meet with	לְהִפָּעֵל (le-hipa'el)	נפעל
לְהִתְאַמֵּץ - To try hard	לְהִתְפַּעֵל (le-hitpa'el)	התפעל

Infinitives can be used in various ways:

- **As nouns:** לְשַׂחֵק (lisḥak) - to play (as a noun) (similar to the gerund 'playing' as a noun, as in "They enjoy playing".

- **With verbs:** אֲנִי אוֹהֵב לִקְרֹא (ani ohev li-k'roa) - "I love to read".

- **With prepositions:** בְּעֵת לִנְטֹע (be'et li-ntoa) - "A time of planting".

Infinitives often (but not always) end with the letter ת (Tav). The infinitive form of a verb can be used as the root for other binyanim. Pay attention to the prefixes and patterns to master infinitive usage in different contexts.

Here's a detailed table for the present tense in פעל (Pa'al), פיעל (Pi'el), הפעיל (Hif'il), נפעל (Nif'al), and התפעל (Hitpa'el) using the root כ-ת-ב (K-T-B, "to write").

Pronoun/Suffix	פעל	פיעל	הפעיל	התפעל	נפעל
Infinitive	לכתוב	לכתב	להכתיב	להתכתב	להיכתב
אני	כותב או כותבת	מכתב	מכתיב או מכתיבה	מתכתב או מתכתבת	נכתב או נכתבת
אתה	כותב	מכתב	מכתיב	מתכתב	נכתב
את	כותבת	מכתבת	מכתיבה	מתכתבת	נכתבת
אנחנו	כותבים או כותבות	מכתבים	מכתיבים או מכתיבות	מתכתבים או מתכתבות	נכתבים או נכתבות

הוא	כותב	מכתב	מכתיב	מתכתב	נכתב
היא	כותבת	מכתבת	מכתיבה	מתכתבת	נכתבת
אתם	כותבים	מכתבים	מכתיבים	מתכתבים	נכתבים
אתן	כותבות	מכתבות	מכתיבות	מתכתבות	נכתבות
הם	כותבים	מכתבים	מכתיבים	מתכתבים	נכתבים
הן	כותבות	מכתבות	מכתיבות	מתכתבות	נכתבות

This table illustrates how the root ב-ת-כ (K-T-B) is conjugated in the present tense for different בניינים and pronouns. It's a key tool for understanding and using the present tense in Hebrew, especially for verbs related to writing and communication.

In Hebrew, roots that end with ה.י.ו (H.Y.V) often undergo a slight modification in their present tense conjugation across different בניינים (Binyanim). Specifically, the final letter ה (He) is usually dropped or replaced when forming present tense verbs. This change applies to verbs in various בניינים, each with its own nuances.

Present Tense Conjugation Table with Example Verbs:

Here's a table illustrating present tense conjugations for specific verbs in different בניינים that follow this pattern:

Binyan	שם פועל	אני	אתה	את	אנחנו	הוא	היא	אתם	אתן	הם	הן
Pa'al	לשחות	שוחה או שוחה	שוחה	שוחה	שוחים או שוחות	שוחה	שוחה	שוחים	שוחות	שוחים	שוחות
Pi'el	לכסות	מכסה או מכסה	מכסה	מכסה	מכסים או מכסות	מכסה	מכסה	מכסים	מכסות	מכסים	מכסות
Hif'il	להקנות	מקנה או מקנה	מקנה	מקנה	מקנים או מקנות	מקנה	מקנה	מקנים	מקנות	מקנים	מקנות
Nif'al	להיראות	נראה או נראית	נראה	נראית	נראים או נראות	נראה	נראית	נראים	נראות	נראים	נראות

This table demonstrates how the root ב-ת-כ (K-T-B) is conjugated in the present tense across different בניינים for various pronouns. It's crucial for understanding and using the present tense in Hebrew, especially for verbs related to writing and communication.

The Four Basic Forms in בניין פעל

These forms can be broken down phonetically into a simple pattern:

- Masculine Singular: O eh
- Feminine Singular: O eh et
- Masculine Plural: O im
- Feminine Plural: O ot

Examples with Different Verbs

Let's apply this pattern to various verbs in פעל בניין. For simplicity, we will use verbs that do not end in ה.

1. **To Write - כותב (Kotev)**
   - כותב (Kotev) - He writes
   - כותבת (Kotevet) - She writes
   - כותבים (Kotvim) - They write (masculine)
   - כותבות (Kotvot) - They write (feminine)

2. **To Eat - אוכל (Ochel)**
   - אוכל (Ochel) - He eats
   - אוכלת (Ochelet) - She eats
   - אוכלים (Ochlim) - They eat (masculine)
   - אוכלות (Ochlot) - They eat (feminine)

3. **To Drink - שותה (Shote)**
   - שותה (Shote) - He drinks
   - שותה (Shota) - She drinks
   - שותים (Shotim) - They drink (masculine)
   - שותות (Shotot) - They drink (feminine)

4. **To Read - קורא (Kore)**
   - קורא (Kore) - He reads
   - קוראת (Kora'at) - She reads
   - קוראים (Kor'im) - They read (masculine)
   - קוראות (Kor'ot) - They read (feminine)

Understanding and applying these patterns will allow you to correctly conjugate a wide range of verbs in the present tense within פעל בניין. As you practice these forms, they will become more intuitive, greatly enhancing your ability to communicate in Hebrew.

Illustrative Table for Present Tense Verbs in פעל בניין

The present tense verbs in פעל בניין (Binyan Pa'al) follow a consistent pattern based on gender and number. Below is a table illustrating these forms using the generic verb פועל (Po'el) as an example:

Gender/Number	Hebrew Verb
Masculine Singular	פועל (Po'el)
Feminine Singular	פועלת (Po'elet)
Masculine Plural	פועלים (Po'alim)
Feminine Plural	פועלות (Po'alot)

Explanation of the Table

- **Masculine Singular (פועל - Po'el)**: This form is used when the subject of the verb is a single male or a general statement is made (when gender is not specified).
- **Feminine Singular (פועלת - Po'elet)**: This form is used for a single female subject.
- **Masculine Plural (פועלים - Po'alim)**: This is used when the subject is multiple males or a mixed-gender group.
- **Feminine Plural (פועלות - Po'alot)**: This form is used for multiple female subjects.

Application with Different שורשים (Roots)

The beauty of Hebrew verbs in פעל בניין is that almost any שורש (Shoresh - root) can be "plugged" into this structure to create verbs. Let's see some examples:

1. שורש: למד (L-M-D, "to learn")
   - לומד (Lomed) - He learns
   - לומדת (Lomedet) - She learns
   - לומדים (Lomdim) - They learn (masculine)
   - לומדות (Lomdot) - They learn (feminine)
2. שורש: רקד (R-K-D, "to dance")

- רוקד (Roked) - He dances
- רוקדת (Rokedet) - She dances
- רוקדים (Rokdim) - They dance (masculine)
- רוקדות (Rokdot) - They dance (feminine)

3. שורש: שמר **(Sh-M-R, "to guard")**
   - שומר (Shomer) - He guards
   - שומרת (Shomeret) - She guards
   - שומרים (Shomrim) - They guard (masculine)
   - שומרות (Shomrot) - They guard (feminine)

Each verb form is derived by applying the specific שורש to the standardized פעל בניין pattern, allowing for a vast array of verbs to be formed with relative ease. Understanding this structure enables learners to quickly expand their Hebrew verb vocabulary and enhances their ability to communicate effectively in various contexts.

Direct Objects

Direct objects are a fundamental aspect of both English and Hebrew grammar, but their treatment in each language has some notable differences.

In English, a direct object is the noun or noun phrase that receives the action of the verb. It answers the question "what?" or "whom?" regarding the action. For example, in the sentence "He threw the ball," the word "ball" is the direct object because it receives the action of "threw."

There are also indirect objects, which indicate to whom or for whom the action is done. For example, in "He threw Lisa the ball," "Lisa" is the indirect object, and "ball" remains the direct object. Prepositional phrases can also be used to indicate direction or recipients, such as in "He threw the ball to Lisa," where "to Lisa" is a prepositional phrase.

In Hebrew, direct objects function similarly in that they receive the action of the verb. However, Hebrew has a unique feature for indicating direct objects: the word את (Et). את precedes the direct object when it is definite (i.e., when it has the definite article "ה").

For instance:

- "He throws the ball" translates to "הכדור את זורק הוא" (Hu zorek et hakedur). Here, "את" (et) is used because "הכדור" (the ball) is a definite direct object.

However, when the direct object is indefinite (without "ה"), את is not used.

- So, "He throws a ball" simply becomes "כדור זורק הוא" (Hu zorek kadur), without את.

The Role of את (Et)

The word את is unique to Hebrew and does not have a direct equivalent in English. It acts as a marker or connector for direct objects that are definite. Its purpose is to clearly distinguish the direct object from other elements of the sentence, making the sentence structure clear and unambiguous.

- "She reads the book" - "היא קוראת את הספר" (Hi koret et hasefer).

Prepositions

Prepositions in Hebrew function similarly to those in English, creating relationships between different elements within a sentence. In this section, we'll focus on two common prepositions: אל (El), meaning "to" or "towards," and עם (Im), meaning "with."

Basic Usage of אל (El) and עם (Im)

- אל (El) is used to indicate direction or destination. It's similar to "to" or "towards" in English.
- עם (Im) is used to indicate accompaniment or association, much like "with" in English.

The Contraction of "אל" (to)

In everyday Hebrew, the preposition "אל" (meaning "to" or "towards") can sometimes be contracted and written as "ל". This occurs mostly in spoken language and informal writing. It's a way of making speech flow more smoothly.

The contraction mainly happens when "אל" precedes a word starting with the definite article "ה" (the). That "ה" sound tends to blend with the "אל", making it sound like "ל".

- **Correct but Formal:** אני הולך אל החוף (Ani holech el ha'chof) - I'm going to the beach.
- **Contracted and Common:** אני הולך לחוף (Ani holech la'chof) - I'm going to the beach (same meaning).

Most of the time, you'll see "ל" instead of "אל" even without the definite article:

- The contraction is considered less formal. In writing that aims for a higher register (essays, official documents), it's safer to stick with the full "אל".
- There isn't a strict rule to always contract "אל". Sometimes it just sounds more natural in its full form, even in casual contexts.

These prepositions will be conjugated in a later chapter, but for now, we'll focus on their basic forms. Here's a table of common Hebrew prepositions and their meanings:

Hebrew Preposition	English Translation	Example Sentence
אחר	After	אחר הארוחה הלכנו לטייל. (After the meal, we went for a walk.)
מאחורי	Behind	אני עומד מאחוריך. (I'm standing behind you.)
אל	To	אל תדאג. (Don't worry.)
אצל	At (with people)	אצל מי אתה גר? (Who do you live with?)

את	To (with objects)	את הספר הזה קראתי כבר. (I already read this book.)
ב	In, At	בים יש דגים. (There are fish in the sea.)
בגלל	Because of	בגלל הגשם, לא הלכנו לבית הספר. (Because of the rain, we didn't go to school.)
בין	Between	בין שני ההרים יש עמק. (There is a valley between the two mountains.)
בלי	Without	בלי כסף אי אפשר לקנות כלום. (You can't buy anything without money.)
בשביל	For (the sake of)	בשבילך אני מוכן לעשות הכל. (I'm ready to do anything for you.)
בתוך	Inside	בתוך הבית חם ונעים. (It's warm and cozy inside the house.)
כ	Like	היא יפה כמו פרח. (She's beautiful like a flower.)
כמו	Like	כמו שאמרתי לך, זה לא פשוט. (Like I told you, it's not simple.)
ל	To	אני הולך לים. (I'm going to the sea.)

לגבי	Regarding	לגבי העבודה, יש לי כמה שאלות. (I have a few questions regarding the job.)
ליד	Near	קטן בית יש הים ליד. (There is a small house near the sea.)
על יד	Next to	הספר בית יד על גר אני. (I live next to the school.)
למען	For the sake of	להתפשר צריכים אנחנו ,השלום למען. (For the sake of peace, we need to compromise.)
לפי	According to	ציבוריים במקומות לעשן אסור ,החוק לפי. (According to the law, it's forbidden to smoke in public places.)
לפני	Before	ידיים לשטוף נוהג אני הארוחה לפני. (I usually wash my hands before the meal.)
מן	From	הארץ מן בא אני. (I come from the country.)
מול	Opposite	אני גר מול הים. (I live opposite the sea.)
מעל	Above	מעל העננים יש שמש. (There is sun above the clouds.)
על	On, Over	על השולחן יש ספר. (There is a book on the table.)

מתחת	Under	מתחת לשולחן יש חתול. (There is a cat under the table.)
עד	Until	אני אהיה כאן עד מחר. (I'll be here until tomorrow.)
עם	With	אני הולך עם חברים. (I'm going with friends.)
על ידי	By means of	על ידי עבודה קשה אפשר להשיג הכל. (By means of hard work, you can achieve anything.)
של	Of	זה הספר של אחי. (This is my brother's book.)

Examples with Sports and Traveling

Here are several examples using אל (El), עם (Im), and the direct object marker את (Et) in the context of sports and traveling, along with verbs in בניין פעל.

1. **Traveling to a Game:**
   o "הוא נוסע למשחק" (Hu nosea lemis'hak) - "He is traveling to the game."
2. **Players Throwing Balls:**
   o "השחקנים זורקים כדורים" (Hashachkanim zorkim kadurim) - "The players are throwing balls."
3. **The Goalkeeper is Good:**
   o "השוער טוב" (Hasho'ar tov) - "The goalkeeper is good."
4. **Dan Sitting with Lisa:**
   o "דן יושב עם ליסה" (Dan yoshev im Lisa) - "Dan is sitting with Lisa."
5. **The Player Throws the Ball to Mati:**
   o "השחקן זורק את הכדור אל מתי" (Hashachkan zorek et hakedur el Mati) - "The player throws the ball to Mati."

6. **Amit Listening to the Television:**
   - "הטלוויזיה את שומע עמית" (Amit shomea et hateleviziyah) - "Amit is listening to the television."

7. **Traveling with Friends:**
   - "חברים עם נוסעת היא" (Hi nosa'at im chaverim) - "She is traveling with friends."

8. **Watching a Football Match:**
   - "כדורגל במשחק צופים הם" (Hem tzofim bemischak kaduregel) - "They are watching a football match."

9. **Riding Bikes to the Park:**
   - "הפארק אל אופניים על רוכבים הילדים" (Hayeladim rochvim al ofanayim el hapark) - "The children are riding bikes to the park."

10. **Jogging to the Beach:**
    - "החוף אל רצה היא" (Hi ratzah el hachof) - "She is jogging to the beach."

These examples illustrate how the prepositions אל and עם, along with the direct object marker את, are used in various contexts related to sports and traveling. Understanding their usage is crucial for constructing accurate and meaningful sentences in Hebrew.

Chapter Summary

This chapter established the essential foundations for beginning your Hebrew learning journey:

→ **Present Tense:** Explored the present tense and Binyanim, highlighting the consistent patterns across different subjects, both in singular and plural forms.

→ **Direct Objects**: Explained the use of the direct object marker את (Et) in Hebrew and its role in identifying definite direct objects in sentences.

→ **Prepositions**: Introduced basic prepositions, אל (El), meaning "to" or "towards," and עם (Im), meaning "with," and their usage in forming coherent phrases.

Practice

Exercise 1:

Select the correct verb from the word bank and conjugate it according to the gender and number implied by the pronoun in each phrase.

Word Bank

- ללמוד (to learn)

- לכתוב (to write)

- לאכול (to eat)

- לשתות (to drink)

- לרקוד (to dance)

- לשמוע (to listen)

- לרוץ (to run)

- לראות (to see)

Exercises

Fill in the blanks with the appropriately conjugated verb from the word bank.

Phrase with Blank	No.
את(learns) _____	1
הם(write) _____	2
אנחנו(eat) _____	3

_____ (drinks)היא	4
_____ (dance)אתה	5
_____ (listen)הן	6
_____ (runs)הוא	7
_____ (see)אני	8

Exercise 2:

Construct the correct Hebrew sentence for each English phrase, focusing on the correct use of direct objects (את) and prepositions. Use the verbs, pronouns, nouns, and adjectives discussed in our chat.

Here's a word bank providing the meanings of the Hebrew words used in the exercises. This will assist in understanding and translating the phrases correctly.

Translate the following English phrases into Hebrew:

English Translation			**Hebrew Word**
Throws	זורק	Watching	צופים
Ball	כדור	Game	משחק
Likes	אוהב	Writing	כותבת
To read	לקרוא	Letters	מכתבים
Books	ספרים	Friends	חברים

With	עם	See	רואים
John	יונתן	Trees	עצים
Dog	כלב	Tall	גבוהים
Big	גדול	Drinks	שותה
Eats; Food	אוכל	Water	מים
Cold	קרים	Dan	דן
Players	שחקנים	Apples	תפוחים
Green	ירוקים	Teacher	מורה
Amit	עמית	Reads	קוראת
		To the students	לתלמידים

No.	English Phrase
1	He throws a ball
2	Dana likes to read books with John
3	The big dog eats the food

4	They are watching the game
5	Lisa is writing letters to her friends
6	The children see the tall trees
7	She drinks the cold water
8	The players are throwing the green balls
9	Amit and Dan are eating apples
10	The teacher reads the book to the students

Chapter 3 Answer Key

Exercise 1:

No.	Correct Phrase
1	את לומדת
2	הם כותבים
3	אנחנו אוכלים
4	היא שותה
5	אתה רוקד
6	הן שומעות
7	הוא רץ
8	אני רואה

Exercise 2:

No.	Hebrew Translation
1	הוא זורק כדור
2	דנה אוהבת לקרוא ספרים עם יונתן
3	הכלב הגדול אוכל את האוכל

Coming up...

In the next chapter, we will delve into the fascinating world of Hebrew preposition conjugation, exploring how prepositions change to match the subjects they are associated with. We'll tackle phrases like "I have" and "You don't have," using the Hebrew words יש (yesh) and אין (ein) and learn how to express possession and absence in different contexts. Additionally, we'll explore how to use את (et) in direct object constructions with different pronouns.

Chapter 4 – Having & Conjugations

With languages, you are at home anywhere.

עִם שָׂפוֹת, אַתָּה בַּבַּיִת בְּכָל מָקוֹם

This chapter gives you some seriously useful building blocks for Hebrew! We're tackling how to say what you have (or don't have), plus a powerful little word that gets you anywhere – literally and figuratively.

"יש" (Yesh) and "אין" (Ein): The Basics

Think of these as the "I have" and "I don't have" of Hebrew. With these words, you can say things like:

- יש לי אח - I have a brother.

- אין לי עט - I do not have a pen.

But it's not just about possessions; these words describe what exists in the world around you! The preposition "ל" (to) is like a compass for your sentences. Want to say "to the store," "to him," or "to my house"? This little word needs to change the form for who or what you're talking about. That's what conjugation is all about! We'll cover forms like:

Conjugation Practice

The little words "את" (Et) and "עם" (Im/It) are integral to correct Hebrew. Get this right, and your sentences will instantly sound more natural!

Conjugated "את"	Object Pronoun	Example
אותי (Oti)	Me	הוא אוהב אותי - He loves me

אוֹתָךְ (Otach)	You (fem.)	אני שומע אותך - I hear you
אוֹתְךָ (Otcha)	You (male.)	הם רוצים אותך - They want you
אוֹתוֹ (Oto)	Him	הם רואים אותו - They see him
אוֹתָה (Ota)	Her	אני קוראת אותה - I'm calling here
אוֹתָנוּ (Otanu)	Us	היא צריכה אותנו - She needs us
אֶתְכֶם (Etchem)	You (pl. masc.)	אנחנו אוהבים אתכם - We need you
אֶתְכֶן (Etchen)	You (pl. fem.)	אני רואה אתכן - I see you
אוֹתָם (Otam)	Them (masc.)	הוא שונא אותם - He hates them
אוֹתָן (Otan)	Them (fem.)	היא מבינה אותן - She understands them

Conjugations for עם (Im/It): In spoken Hebrew, עם is often conjugated as אית (It) when combined with pronouns. Examples in Sentences:

Conjugated	With Pronoun
אִיתִי	Me
אִיתְךָ	You (masc.)

איתך	You (fem.)
איתו	Him
איתה	Her
איתנו	Us
איתכם	You (pl. masc.)
איתכן	You (pl. fem.)
איתם	Them (masc.)
איתן	Them (fem.)

Table of ל Conjugations

Here's how "ל" is conjugated with different pronouns:

Pronoun	Conjugated ל	Example
Me	לִי	הוא נותן לי מתנה - He is giving me a gift
You (masculine, singular)	לְךָ	אני כותב לך מכתב - I am writing you a letter
You (feminine, singular)	לָךְ	אני קורא לך - I am calling you

Him	לו	אני אומר לו את זה - I am telling him this
Her	לה	אני מסביר לה - I am explaining to her
Us	לנו	הם שולחים לנו הודעה - They are sending us a message
You (masculine, plural)	לכם	אני מביא לכם עוגה - I am bringing you a cake
You (feminine, plural)	לכן	אני מספר לכן משהו - I am teling you something
Them (masculine)	להם	אני עוזר להם - I am helping them
Them (feminine)	להן	אני מדבר אליהן - I am speaking to them

Sometimes "ל" with "the" (ה) sounds like "la", especially in casual speech.

To have or not to have

Here's an improved version of the text:

Mastering "Yesh" (יש) and "Ein" (אין): Expressing Possession and Absence

In Hebrew, "Yesh" (יש) and "Ein" (אין) are two essential words that allow you to express having and not having something, respectively. These words are used frequently in everyday conversation, so mastering their conjugations is crucial for building accurate and natural-sounding sentences.

Conjugation Tables:

Here are the conjugations for "Yesh" (יש) and "Ein" (אין) based on the subject: **Using "Yesh" (יש) and "Ein" (אין) with Food**

Now let's put "Yesh" (יש) and "Ein" (אין) to work in sentences with food items and adjectives:

Pronoun	Not having	Having
I	אין לי (Ein Li)	יש לי
You (masc.)	אין לך (Ein L'cha)	יש לך
You (fem.)	אין לך (Ein Lach)	יש לך
He	אין לו (Ein Lo)	יש לו
She	אין לה	יש לה
We	אין לנו	יש לנו
You (pl. masc)	אין לכם	יש לכם
You (pl. fem.)	אין לכן	יש לכן
They (masc.)	אין להם	יש להם
They (fem.)	אין להן	יש להן

- **He has a big kitchen:** "יש לו מטבח גדול" (Yesh lo mitbach gadol).

- **We don't have pizza:** "אין לנו פיצה" (Ein lanu pizza).

- **She has delicious fruit:** "יש לה פירות טעימים" (Yesh lah peirot ta'imim).

- **I don't have a cold drink:** "אין לי משקה קר" (Ein li mashkeh kar).

- **They have fresh vegetables:** "יש להם ירקות טריים" (Yesh lahem yerakot tariyim).

- **You (fem.) have a small dining room:** "יש לך חדר אוכל קטן" (Yesh lach chadar ochel katan).

- **You (pl. masc.) don't have hot soup:** "אין לכם מרק חם" (Ein lachem marak cham).

- **I have a new oven:** "יש לי תנור חדש" (Yesh li tanur chadash).

- **The children have sweet candy:** "יש לילדים סוכריות מתוקות" (Yesh layeladim sukarriot metukot).

- **Dan and Lisa don't have bread for the sandwich:** "אין לדן ולליסה לחם לכריך" (Ein leDan uleLisa lechem lakarich).

Chapter Summary

This chapter established the essential foundations for beginning your Hebrew learning journey:

→ **Conjugations**: Delved into the conjugations of prepositions, particularly "עם" (Im/It) in its spoken form and "את" (Et), demonstrating how these words change based on the subject or object they are associated with.

→ **Having and not Having:** Introduced the concepts of "יש" (Yesh) and "אין" (Ein), which are used to express possession and absence.

Practice

Exercise 1:

This exercise is designed to help you practice conjugating the prepositions את (Et), עם (Im/It), ל (Le), and אל (El) in various contexts. You will choose the correct conjugated form based on the given subject.

1. Determine the subject in each sentence.
2. Choose the correct conjugated form of את, עם, ל, or אל from the options provided.

No.	Sentence with Blank	English
1	היא קוראת _____ ספר	She is reading them a book.
2	הוא רוצה ללכת ____ הקונצרט	He wants to go to the concert.
3	אנחנו מביאים _____ מתנה	We are bringing you a gift.
4	הם משחקים כדורגל _____	They are playing football (soccer) with us.
5	את צריכה לדבר _____	You need to talk with him.
6	הם רואים _____ התמונה	They see the picture.
7	דן מספר סיפור ____ילדים	Dan is telling a story to the children.
8	אני אוכל צהריים ___ אמא	I am having lunch with mom.
9	היא מחפשת ___ החולצה	She's looking for the shirt.

10   יש לי פגישה ___ דנה   I have a meeting with Dana.

Exercise 2:

Complete the sentences by choosing the correct form of "יש" or "אין" along with the appropriate pronoun.

Exercise Table

English	Sentence with Blank	No.
I have a ticket to the concert.	כרטיס לקונצרט_____	1
She doesn't have a new book.	ספר חדש _____	2
We have a good idea.	רעיון טוב _____	3
They (fem.) are out of time (they do not have time).	זמן _____	4
You (masc.) have an opportunity.	הזדמנות_____	5
He has an answer to that question.	תשובה לשאלה_____	6
You have a solution to the problem.	פתרון לבעיה _____	7
I don't have the car keys.	מפתחות המכונית_____	8
They have tickets to the game.	כרטיסים למשחק_____	9

You have a desire to learn.   חשק ללמוד_____   10

Exercise 3:

Practice transforming sentences between having ("יש") and not having ("אין"), and vice versa, while incorporating שמות פעולה (infinitives) to create pseudo-complex sentences. Transform each sentence from "יש" to "אין" or from "אין" to "יש" and make necessary adjustments to the rest of the sentence. Pay attention to the infinitive forms of the verbs. Afterwards, translate the transformed sentences into English, using the **word bank**:

Hebrew Word	English Translation	Hebrew Word	English Translation
הזדמנות	Opportunity	זמן	Time
לטייל	To travel	ללמוד	To learn
בחו"ל	Abroad	עברית	Hebrew
עניין	Interest	כרטיסים	Tickets
ללמוד	To learn	להופעה	To the show
גיטרה	Guitar	רצון	Desire, Want

חשק	Desire, Wish	לשחק	To play
לעזור	To help	כדורגל	Soccer
מטבח	Kitchen	כסף	Money
תוכניות	Plans	לקנות	To buy
סוף השבוע	Weekend	מחשב	Computer
זמן	Time	חדש	New
לראות	To see	תשובה	Answer
סרט	Movie	שאלה	Question
כל	All	מספיק	Enough

Transformed Sentence	Original Sentence	No.
	יש להם זמן ללמוד עברית	1

Chapter 4 Answer Key

Exercise 1:

No.	Correct Conjugation
1	להם
2	אל הקונצרט / לקונצרט
3	לך / לכם / לכן
4	איתנו
5	איתו
6	את
7	לילדים / אל הילדים
8	עם
9	את
10	עם

Exercise 2:

Correct Sentence	No.
יש לי כרטיס לקונצרט	1

אין לה ספר חדש	2
יש לנו רעיון טוב	3
אין להן זמן	4
יש לכם הזדמנות	5
יש לו תשובה לשאלה	6
יש לך פתרון לבעיה	7
אין לי מפתחות המכונית	8
יש להם כרטיסים למשחק	9
יש לך חשק ללמוד	10

Exercise 3:

English Translation	Correct Transformed Sentence	No.
They don't have time to learn Hebrew.	אין להם זמן ללמוד עברית	1
I have tickets to the show.	יש לי כרטיסים להופעה	2
He doesn't want to play soccer.	אין לו רצון לשחק כדורגל	3

We have enough money to buy a new computer.	יש לנו מספיק כסף לקנות מחשב חדש	4
She doesn't have an answer to every question.	אין לה תשובה לכל שאלה	5
You have the opportunity to travel abroad.	יש לכם הזדמנות לטייל בחו"ל	6
I am not interested in learning guitar.	אין לי עניין ללמוד גיטרה	7
She wants to help in the kitchen.	יש לה חשק לעזור במטבח	8
We have no plans for the weekend.	אין לנו תוכניות לסוף השבוע	9
You have time to watch a movie.	יש לך זמן לראות סרט	10

Coming up...

In the next chapter, we will dive into the world of numbers in Hebrew. We'll explore cardinal and ordinal numbers, learn how to count, and practice using numbers in real-life scenarios.

Chapter 5 – Numbers

The limits of my language mean the limits of my world.

גְּבוּלוֹת שְׂפָתַי הֵם גְּבוּלוֹת עוֹלָמִי

Mastering numbers is key for everyday Hebrew communication! This chapter unveils some unique features of Hebrew:

- **Number Genders:** Numbers change form to match the noun they describe (masculine or feminine). Learn this for accurate counting and descriptions.
- **"כמה" (Kamah):** This versatile word means "how many" or "how much." We'll use it to ask essential questions about quantity.
- **Practical Applications:** We'll focus on how numbers are used when talking about money (shopping, dining) and telling time – skills you use daily.

By the end, you'll be confidently employing Hebrew numbers in real conversations. Get ready to count, ask, and tell like a pro!

Numbers

Here's a comprehensive look at Hebrew numbers, covering from 1 to 20 in both masculine and feminine forms, followed by tens, hundreds, and higher numbers. Note that in Hebrew, numbers often take different forms depending on whether they are masculine or feminine.

Feminine	Masculine	Number
אחת (Achat)	אחד (Echad)	1
שתיים (Shtayim)	שניים (Shnayim)	2

שלוש (Shalosh)	שלושה (Shlosha)	3
ארבע (Arba)	ארבעה (Arba'a)	4
חמש (Chamesh)	חמישה (Chamisha)	5
שש (Shesh)	שישה (Shisha)	6
שבע (Sheva)	שבעה (Shiv'a)	7
שמונה (Shmoneh)	שמונה (Shmona)	8
תשע (Tesha)	תשעה (Tisha)	9
עשר (Eser)	עשרה (Asara)	10
אחת עשרה (Achat Esreh)	אחד עשר (Achad Asar)	11
שתים עשרה (Shtaim Esreh)	שנים עשר (Shneim Asar)	12
שלוש עשרה (Shalosh Esreh)	שלושה עשר (Shlosha Asar)	13
ארבע עשרה (Arba Esreh)	ארבעה עשר (Arba'a Asar)	14
חמש עשרה (Chamesh Esreh)	חמישה עשר (Chamisha Asar)	15
שש עשרה (Shesh Esreh)	שישה עשר (Shisha Asar)	16
שבע עשרה (Sheva Esreh)	שבעה עשר (Shiv'a Asar)	17
שמונה עשרה (Shmoneh Esreh)	שמונה עשר (Shmona Asar)	18

	Number
תשע עשרה (Tesha Esreh)	תשעה עשר (Tisha Asar) 19
עשרים (Esrim)	עשרים (Esrim) 20

Masculine & Feminine	Number
שלושים (Shloshim)	30
ארבעים (Arba'im)	40
חמישים (Chamishim)	50
שישים (Shishim)	60
שבעים (Shiv'im)	70
שמונים (Shmonim)	80
תשעים (Tish'im)	90
מאה (Mea)	100
מאתיים (Matayim)	200
שלוש מאות (Shlosh Meot)	300
ארבע מאות (Arba Meot)	400
חמש מאות (Chamesh Meot)	500

שש מאות (Shesh Meot)	600
שבע מאות (Sheva Meot)	700
שמונה מאות (Shmoneh Meot)	800
תשע מאות (Tisha Meot)	900
אלף (Elef)	1,000
אלפיים (Alpayim)	2,000
מיליון (Milyon)	1,000,000

Hebrew numbers have unique characteristics and a few exceptions that are important to understand. Here's a breakdown with some tips to help you remember and use them correctly.

Exceptions and Gender Agreement

- מאתיים **(Matayim)** and אלפיים **(Alpayim)**: These are the words for 200 and 2000, respectively, and are exceptions in their form. Unlike other numbers, they do not follow the regular pattern of adding the word for 'hundred' or 'thousand' after the number.

- מאה **(Mea)**: The word for 100 is feminine, which is why we say שלוש מאות **(Shlosh Meot)** for 300 and not שלושה מאות. This gender agreement is crucial for numbers in the hundreds.

- שלושה **(Shlosha)** vs. שלוש **(Shalosh)**: Though it might seem counterintuitive, שלושה is masculine, and שלוש is feminine. A helpful tip is to remember that the shorter word (שלוש) is feminine - less is more feminine!

- **Numbers 1 and 2**: These are the only numbers where the masculine and feminine forms are completely different words (אחד/אחת, שניים/שתיים). From 3 upwards, the forms are more similar.

Creating Numbers Like 21, 43, 145, and 940

- **21, 43, etc.:** These numbers are formed by combining the word for the tens and then the word for the unit. For example, 21 is ואחת עשרים (Esrim Ve'achat) for feminine nouns and ואחד עשרים (Esrim Ve'echad) for masculine nouns. 43 is ושלוש ארבעים (Arba'im Ve'shalosh) for feminine and ושלושה ארבעים (Arba'im Ve'shlosha) for masculine.

- **145, 940, etc.:** Larger numbers like these are created by stating the hundreds, then the tens, and finally the units. For example, 145 is וחמש ארבעים מאה (Mea Arba'im Ve'chamesh) for feminine nouns, and 940 is ארבעים מאות תשע (Tisha Meot Arba'im) for both masculine and feminine (as there is no unit number).

How many

Understanding how to discuss money is crucial in Hebrew, especially if you're visiting Israel or dealing with financial matters. The primary currency in Israel is the Shekel (שקל, pronounced 'Shekel'), and its smaller denomination is Agurot (אגורות, pronounced 'Agurot').

- שקל **(Shekel)**: The basic unit of currency in Israel.

- אגורות **(Agurot)**: 100 Agurot make up one Shekel, similar to cents in a dollar.

- דולר **(Dollar)**: The American currency is also commonly referred to in Israel.

Asking "How Many" and "How Much Does This Cost":

כמה **(Kamah)**: This word means "how many" or "how much". It's used for asking about quantity or price.

- Asking about quantity: עולה זה כמה? **(Kamah zeh oleh?)** - "How much does this cost?"

- Asking about money: שקלים כמה? **(Kamah shekalim?)** - "How many shekels?"

Examples with Money:

1. "כמה עולה הקפה? עשרה שקלים."

("Kamah oleh hakahfeh? Asarah shekalim.") - "How much is the coffee? Ten shekels."

2. "התפוזים עולים חמישה שקלים לקילו."

("Hatapuzim olim chamesh shekalim lekilo.") - "The oranges cost five shekels per kilo."

3. "הנסיעה לשדה התעופה עולה מאה שקלים."

("Hanesi'ah lasde hate'ufah oleh meah shekalim.") - "The ride to the airport costs one hundred shekels."

4. "כמה זה עולה? עשרים וחמש שקלים."

("Kamah zeh oleh? Esrim ve'chamesh shekalim.") - "How much does this cost? Twenty-five shekels."

Time of day

Understanding the structure and vocabulary for telling time will help you in everyday conversations, from scheduling meetings to social arrangements.

- מה השעה?

(Mah HaSha'ah?): "What time is it?"

- השעה...

(HaSha'ah...): "It is... o'clock."

In Hebrew, time is generally told on a 12-hour clock, with an indication of whether it's morning or evening.

- בוקר

(Boker): Morning

- ערב

(Erev): Evening

o השעה שש

(HaSha'ah shesh) - "It is six o'clock."

o השעה חמש ועשר

(HaSha'ah chamesh ve'eser) - "It is ten past five."

o השעה שבע ועשרים

(HaSha'ah sheva ve'esrim) - "It is twenty past seven."

o עשרים לשש

(Esrim le'shesh) - "Twenty to six."

o רבע לשבע

(Reva le'sheva) - "Quarter to seven."

o שש בבוקר

(Shesh ba'boker) - "Six in the morning."

o שמונה בערב

(Shmoneh ba'erev) - "Eight in the evening."

This table summarizes common time-related words and expressions in Hebrew, essential for daily communication.

Hebrew Expression	English Expression
מה השעה?(Mah HaSha'ah?) ?	What time is it?
כמה זמן יש?(Kamah zman yesh?) ?	How much time is there?
רבע ל[שעה](Reva le[sha'ah])]	Quarter to [hour]
שתיים וחצי(Shtayim uchetzi)	Half past two
שעה(Sha'ah)	Hour
שעתיים(Shtey sha'ot)	Two hours
שתי דקות(Shtey dakot)	2 minutes
חמש דקות(Chamesh dakot)	5 minutes
רבע שעה(Reva sha'ah)	Quarter of an hour
יום(Yom)	Day
יומיים(Yomayim)	Two days

שבוע(Shavu'a)	Week
חודש(Chodesh)	Month
שבועיים(Shvu'ayim)	Two weeks
חודשיים(Chodshayim)	Two months
חצי שעה(Chatzi sha'ah)	Half an hour

Chapter Summary

This chapter established the essential foundations for beginning your Hebrew learning journey:

→ **Numbers**: Introduced both the masculine and feminine forms of Hebrew numbers, covering from 1 to 1 million.

→ **How many:** Explored the usage of "כמה" (Kamah) for asking about quantities and amounts, which is essential for inquiring about and understanding quantities in various contexts, from shopping to scheduling.

→ **Money**: Covered the basics of talking about money in Hebrew, including the terms for the Israeli currency (Shekels and Agurot), and how to discuss prices and financial transactions.

→ **What time is it**: Focused on telling and asking for the time in Hebrew, using a range of time-related vocabulary and expressions, from specific times of the day to durations and periods.

Practice

Exercise 1:

This exercise involves forming Hebrew sentences that answer questions about quantities. The answer box includes a specific number, and your task is to write out the full sentence in Hebrew, correctly expressing the number.

Answer Box (Number Format)	Question	No.
5	כמה ספרים יש לך? (How many books do you have?)	1
3	כמה תפוחים יש לה? (How many apples does she have?)	2
10	כמה חולצות יש לו? (How many shirts does he have?)	3
4	כמה כדורים יש לילדים? (How many balls do the children have?)	4
20	כמה כוסות מים יש לנו? (How many glasses of water do we have?)	5
2	כמה כלבים יש לך? (How many dogs do you have?)	6
7	כמה שעות יש לה פנאי? (How many hours of free time does she have?)	7
15	כמה מחשבים יש במשרד? (How many computers are there in the office?)	8
7	כמה ימים יש בשבוע? (How many days are in a week?)	9

6	How many chairs are in the) כמה כיסאות יש בחדר? (room?)	10

Exercise 2:

Correct Sentence in Hebrew	No.
יש לי חמישה ספרים (I have five books.)	1
יש לה שלושה תפוחים (She has three apples.)	2
יש לו עשר חולצות (He has ten shirts.)	3
יש לילדים ארבעה כדורים (The children have four balls.)	4
יש לנו עשרים כוסות מים (We have twenty glasses of water.)	5
יש לי שני כלבים (I have two dogs.)	6
יש לה שבע שעות פנאי (She has seven hours of free time.)	7
יש במשרד חמשה עשר מחשבים (There are fifteen computers in the office.)	8
יש שבעה ימים בשבוע (There are seven days in a week.)	9
יש ששה כיסאות בחדר (There are six chairs in the room.)	10

Chapter 5 Answer Key

Exercise 1:

No.	Correct Sentence in Hebrew
1	יש לי חמישה ספרים (I have five books.)
2	יש לה שלושה תפוחים (She has three apples.)
3	יש לו עשר חולצות (He has ten shirts.)
4	יש לילדים ארבעה כדורים (The children have four balls.)
5	יש לנו עשרים כוסות מים (We have twenty glasses of water.)
6	יש לי שני כלבים (I have two dogs.)
7	יש לה שבע שעות פנאי (She has seven hours of free time.)
8	יש במשרד חמשה עשר מחשבים (There are fifteen computers in the office.)
9	יש שבעה ימים בשבוע (There are seven days in a week.)
10	יש ששה כיסאות בחדר (There are six chairs in the room.)

Exercise 2:

No.	Correct Time in Hebrew
1	רבע אחרי שמונה בבוקר - "Quarter past eight in the morning."

2   שלוש אחר הצהריים - "Three in the afternoon."

3   עשר דקות לשבע בערב - "Ten to seven in the evening."

4   שתים וחצי אחר הצהריים - "Half past twelve in the afternoon."

5   חמש וחמש דקות בבוקר - "Five oh five in the morning."

6   עשרים דקות לעשר בערב - "Twenty to ten in the evening."

7   עשרים וחמש דקות אחרי שתיים בצהריים - "Twenty-five past two in the afternoon."

8   רבע אחרי אחת עשרה בלילה - "Quarter past eleven at night."

9   חמש דקות לחמש בערב - "Five to five in the evening."

10   שעה אחת לפנות בוקר - "One o'clock at night."

Coming up...

In the next chapter, we will explore more prepositions and question words, enhancing your ability to construct meaningful queries and responses. Additionally, we will cover the concept of possession, learning how to use terms like שלי (sheli - mine), שלך (shelcha/shelach - yours), and more.

Chapter 6 – Question Words, Prepositions, Possession

A different language is a different vision of life.

שָׂפָה אַחֶרֶת הִיא חָזוֹן אַחֵר שֶׁל הַחַיִּים

We'll start this chapter by exploring the conjugations of commonly used prepositions:

- בְ **(In/With)**

- מְ **(From)**

These prepositions are fundamental in Hebrew and conjugate according to the pronouns they accompany, allowing for more precise and varied expressions. The conjugations for these prepositions will be explored below.

Question Words

Understanding question words is key to effective communication. We'll cover the most commonly used Hebrew question words and their usage:

- מתי **(Matai)** - When

- איך **(Eich)** - How

- למה **(Lamah)** - Why

- מי **(Mi)** - Who

- מה **(Mah)** - What

- איפה **(Eifo)** - Where

- איזה **(Eize)** - Which

- מאיפה **(Me'ayfo)** - From where

- לאן **(Le'an)** - To where

Possession (של)

The concept of possession in Hebrew is expressed with the word "של" (Shel). This chapter will teach you how to use "של" to indicate belonging, along with its appropriate conjugations:

- שלי **(Sheli)** - Mine

- שלך **(Shelcha/Shelach)** - Yours (masculine/feminine)

- שלו **(Shelo)** - His

- שלה **(Shelah)** - Hers

- שלנו **(Shelanu)** - Ours

- שלכן/שלכם **(Shelachem/Shelachen)** - Yours (plural masculine/feminine)

- שלהן/שלהם **(Shelahem/Shelahen)** - Theirs (masculine/feminine)

Hebrew Question Words

Question Word	Definition	Example Use
איפה (Eifo)	Where	איפה המסעדה? -"Where is the restaurant?"
לאן (Le'an)	To Where	לאן אתה הולך? -"Where are you going?"
מאיפה (Me'ayfo)	From Where	מאיפה הגעת? -"Where did you come from?"

למה (Lamah)	Why	"Why are you crying?" -?למה אתה בוכה
איך (Eich)	How	"How to get to the station?" -?איך להגיע לתחנה
מתי (Matai)	When	"When is the meeting?" -?מתי הפגישה
מי (Mi)	Who	"Who is that?" - ?מי זה
מה (Mah)	What	"What is that on the table?" - ?מה זה על השולחן
איזה (Eize)	Which	"Which book do you want?" - ?איזה ספר אתה רוצה

Asking for directions in Hebrew combines question words with directional vocabulary. Master these to navigate like a pro!

Directional Words

Transliteration	Hebrew	English
Tzafon	צפון	North
Darom	דרום	South
Mizrach	מזרח	East
Ma'arav	מערב	West
Smol	שמאל	Left

Yamin	ימין	Right
Ma'alah	מעלה	Up
Matah	מטה	Down
Lifnot	לפנות	To turn
Yashar	ישר	Straight

Example Questions

English Translation	Hebrew Example
Which way is north?	?איזה דרך לצפון
How do you arrive at the train station?	?איך מגיעים לתחנת הרכבת
When do I need to turn right?	?מתי אני צריך לפנות ימינה
Is this straight the whole way?	?האם זה ישר כל הדרך
To where to I turn to the museum?	?לאן אני פונה למוזיאון
Where is the closest supermarket?	?איפה הסופרמרקט הקרוב
Does this elevator go down?	?האם המעלית פה מובילה מטה

Prepositions in Hebrew: Mastering "בְּ" (be) and "מִ" (me)

Introduction

Prepositions are small words that establish relationships between other words in a sentence. Mastering the prepositions "בְּ" (be – in/at) and "מִ" (me – from) is essential for building clear and accurate Hebrew sentences.

בְּ (Be) - "In" or "At"

- **Meaning:** Indicates location or state.
- **Conjugations:** "בְּ" changes form depending on the pronoun it accompanies.

Conjugated "בְּ" (be)	Pronoun
בִּי	I
בְּךָ	You (masc.)
בָּךְ	You (fem.)
בּוֹ	He
בָּה	She
בָּנוּ	We

	בכם	You (pl. masc.)
	בכן	You (pl. fem.)
	בהם	They (masc.)
	בהן	They (fem.)

(Me) - "From"

English Translation	Example	Conjugated "מ" (me)	Pronoun
The letter is from me.	המכתב ממני	ממני	I
I received a gift from you.	קיבלתי מתנה ממך	ממך	You (masc.)
I heard the news from you.	שמעתי את החדשות ממך	ממך	You (fem.)
He came out of it.	הוא יצא ממנו	ממנו	He
She took the child from her.	היא לקחה את הילד ממנה	ממנה	She
They traveled from us.	הם נסעו מאיתנו	מאיתנו/ממנו	We

We received help from you.	קיבלנו עזרה מכם	מכם	You (pl. masc.)
We heard the rumor from you.	שמענו את השמועה מכן	מכן	You (pl. fem.)
They took the book from them.	הם לקחו את הספר מהם	מהם	They (masc.)
They heard the story from them.	הן שמעו את הסיפור מהן	מהן	They (fem.)

Possession

In Hebrew, the word "של" (shel) plays a similar role to "of" or "belonging to" in English. It's used to show who owns something or the relationship between entities.

"של" + **Suffix**	**Pronoun**
שלי	I (me)
שלך	You (masc, singular)
שלך	You (fem, singular)
שלו	He (him)
שלה	She (her)
שלנו	We (us)

שלכם	You (masc., plural)
שלכן	You (fem., plural)
שלהם	They (masc.)
שלהן	They (fem.)

To ask "whose" something is, use the following:

- **(Shel mi zeh?)** - Whose is this? (masculine objects)?של מי זה
- **(Shel mi zot?)** - Whose is this? (feminine objects)?של מי זאת

Examples

- **Ownership:** "הבית שלי" (Ha'bayit sheli) - My house

- **Relationship** "החבר שלה" (Ha'chaver shelah) - Her boyfriend

- **Question:** "?של מי המפתחות האלה" (Shel mi ha'maftechot ha'eleh?) - Whose are these keys?

Chapter Summary

→ **Question Words**: Explored various Hebrew question words like מתי (Matai - when), איך (Eich - how), למה (Lamah - why), and others, essential for forming a wide range of questions.

→ **Prepositions:** Delved into the advanced usage and conjugation of key prepositions like ב (Be - in), מ (Me - from), and their variations, crucial for describing locations, movements, and relationships in sentences.

→ **Possession**: Covered the concept of possession using של (Shel), including its conjugations like שלי (Sheli - mine), שלך (Shelcha/Shelach - yours), etc., to express ownership and belonging.

Practice

Exercise 1:

This exercise is designed to help you practice using the correct Hebrew question words in sentences. Your task is to fill in the blank with the appropriate question word. Use the full English version provided as a reference point.

Full English Version	Sentence with Blank (Hebrew)	No.
Where are the restrooms?	_____ השירותים?	1
Where do you want to go tonight?	_____ אתה רוצה ללכת הערב?	2
Why does it hurt?	_____ זה כואב?	3
Did you do the homework?	_____ עשית את השיעורי בית?	4
How did you get here?	_____ הגעת לפה?	5
When is the party?	_____ המסיבה?	6
Where did you buy this car?	_____ קנית את המכונית הזו?	7
How are you feeling now?	_____ אתה מרגיש עכשיו?	8
What is this?	_____ זה?	9
What is your name?	_____ קוראים לך?	10

Exercise 2:

English Reference	Sentence with Blank (Hebrew)	No.
I am talking to you (fem.)	אני מדברת (_____) (to)	1
I want to go to the cinema with them (masc.)	אני רוצה ללכת _____ (to) הקולנוע	2
This letter comes from the CEO	המכתב הזה בא _____ (from) המנכ"ל	3
I have a meeting with the doctor	יש לי פגישה _____ (with) הרופא	4
The books are in the library	הספרים נמצאים _____ (in) הספרייה	5
Thank you for the gift from you (masc.)	תודה על המתנה _____ (from) אותך	6
We are meeting with the teacher	אנחנו נפגשים _____ (with) המורה	7
He is coming from the big city	הוא מגיע _____ (from) העיר הגדולה	8
I bought it in a shop	קניתי את זה _____ (in) חנות	9
You can go to the kitchen	אתה יכול ללכת _____ (to) המטבח	10

Chapter 6 Answer Key

Exercise 1:

English Translation	Correct Sentence in Hebrew	No.
Where are the restrooms?	איפה השירותים?	1
Where do you want to go tonight?	לאן אתה רוצה ללכת הערב?	2
Why does it hurt?	למה זה כואב?	3
Did you do the homework?	מה עשית את השיעורי בית?	4
How did you get here?	איך הגעת לפה?	5
When is the party?	מתי המסיבה?	6
Where did you buy this car?	איפה קנית את המכונית הזו?	7
How are you feeling now?	איך אתה מרגיש עכשיו?	8
What is this?	מה זה?	9
What is your name?	איך קוראים לך?	10

Exercise 2:

English Translation	Correct Sentence in Hebrew	No.

I am talking to you (fem.)	לך אני מדברת	1
I want to go to the cinema with them (masc.)	לקולנוע אני רוצה ללכת איתם	2
This letter comes from the CEO	המכתב הזה בא מהמנכ"ל	3
I have a meeting with the doctor	יש לי פגישה עם הרופא	4
The books are in the library	הספרים נמצאים בספרייה	5
Thank you for the gift from you (masc.)	תודה על המתנה ממך	6
We are meeting with the teacher	אנחנו נפגשים עם המורה	7
He is coming from the big city	הוא מגיע מהעיר הגדולה	8
I bought it in a shop	קניתי את זה בחנות	9
You can go to the kitchen	אתה יכול ללכת למטבח	10

Conclusion

Hebrew, a tongue of ancient roots and fascinating peculiarities, serves as a unique means of communication that opens doors to a captivating and rich culture. Throughout this book, we've journeyed from Hebrew sentence formation to the intriguing world of Hebrew grammar – the *Dikduk*. You've grasped concepts such as 'Binyanim,' roots, and verb conjugation patterns.

The skills you've honed herein provide the essential groundwork for further exploration and mastery. The forthcoming book in this series, focusing on vocabulary expansion and conversational skills, will build upon this strong grammatical foundation. It is designed to advance your rudimentary understanding to a more comprehensive grasp of *spoken* Hebrew.

Leveraging your knowledge of Hebrew grammar, you will be capable of not only dissecting Hebrew sentences but also speaking fluently and immersing yourself fully in Hebrew-speaking milieus. The third book in this series will broaden your vocabulary and enhance your speaking skills, and it introduces a wide range of words and idioms, all rooted in the grammatical knowledge acquired from this second book.

Congratulations on making this step in your journey into Hebrew grammar. Best wishes as you persist in your language journey with the following stages in the series!

BOOK 3

Complete Hebrew Workbook for Adult Beginners: **Speaking**

Speak Hebrew in 30 Days!

Explore to Win

Introduction

מָבוֹא

(MaVo)

Success is not final; failure is not fatal: it is the courage to continue that counts.

הַהַצְלָחָה אֵינָהּ סוֹפִית, הַכִּשָּׁלוֹן אֵינוּ פָּטָלִי: הָאֹמֶץ לְהַמְשִׁיךְ הוּא זֶה שֶׁחָשׁוּב

ברוכים הבאים

Bruchim HaBa'im

(Welcome!)

Congratulations on reaching the final stage of your 30-day Hebrew journey! By now, you've conquered the *Alef-Bet* and mastered essential *Dikduk* (grammar). Think of the first two books as your Hebrew boot camp. You learned many of the basics, got the rules down, and laid the groundwork. Now, it's time to begin putting it into action. In this book, we're focusing on how real Israelis speak every day. Prepare to navigate different situations, play with complex tenses, and get comfortable with the kind of casual, fast-paced Hebrew you'd hear on the streets of Tel Aviv, Jerusalem, or even in Israeli communities in Los Angeles or Las Vegas.

Let's explore a few things you can expect:

- You'll get the full rundown on past and future tenses, giving you the tools to build detailed stories and navigate those Israeli history conversations.
- Think ordering food, navigating directions, or having a casual chat – we'll focus on practical, everyday contexts, giving you usable phrases from day one.
- **Breaking the Ice:** Hypotheticals, questions, and opinions – Prepare to get more creative and opinionated using your growing Hebrew skills. This isn't about rules anymore, it's about self-expression.

- We'll also dive into something I call "**Sababa Speak.**" Ditch the formality and learn Israeli slang and the shortcuts everyone uses. This is all about chatting like a local.

Beyond the Basics

Learning Hebrew inevitably introduces you to the country, culture, and rich history of Israel. The knowledge you'll gain in this final book will open new doors, both as a traveler and as a lover of languages. Learning languages is never effortless. But the feeling of unlocking the secrets of conversation, of understanding humour and cultural references in their original tongue – that's the prize. This last book is where your patience as a student of this language pays off.

Let's Get Started! With every page, you're closing in on that 30-day goal. Ready to have your world (and conversations!) expanded by Hebrew? Let's dive in!

~

Embrace the challenge today.

Experience the joy of speaking Hebrew in just 30 days.

Chapter 1 – "What was, was."

Every great thing starts with one small step.

כָּל דָּבָר גָּדוֹל מַתְחִיל בְּצַעַד אֶחָד קָטָן

Welcome to Chapter 1, where we'll embark on the journey of mastering the past tense in Hebrew across various verbal patterns (בניינים), excluding Pual (פועל) and Hufal (הופעל).

Understanding בניינים in Past Tense

Hebrew verbs are categorized into several patterns known as בניינים (Binyanim), each with its own semantic nuances. In this chapter, we'll cover the past tense in these בניינים:

- **Pa'al** (פָּעַל)

- **Pi'el** (פִּעֵל)

- **Hitpa'el** (הִתְפַּעֵל)

- **Nif'al** (נִפְעַל)

- **Hif'il** (הִפְעִיל)

Each בניין will be explored to understand how it transforms in the past tense.

Consistent Suffixes

Despite the differences in the בניינים, past tense verbs in Hebrew generally follow a pattern of suffixes that correspond to the subject of the verb. These suffixes are critical for conjugating verbs correctly in the past tense:

- **X-תי (ti)** - I (e.g., דיברתי - I spoke)

- **X-נו (nu)** - We (e.g., דיברנו - We spoke)

- **X-ה (a)** - He/She (e.g., דיברה - She spoke)

- **X-ו (u)** - They (e.g., דיברו - They spoke)

- **X-תם (tem)** - You (masculine plural) (e.g., דיברתם - You spoke)

- **X-תן (ten)** - You (feminine plural) (e.g., דיברתן - You spoke)

Use the following conjugations as a prime example of how this structure can work for each Binyan.

Pi'el

Past Tense Conjugation Table for לדבר (L'daber) in Pa'al (פָּעַל)

Pronouns / Pa'al	Conjugation
I (masc. and fem.)	דיברתי (Dibarti)
You (masc. sing.)	דיברת (Dibarta)
You (fem. sing.)	דיברת (Dibart)
He	דיבר (Diber)
She	דיברה (Dibra)
We (masc. and fem.)	דיברנו (Dibarnu)
You (masc. pl.)	דיברתם (Dibartem)
You (fem. pl.)	דיברתן (Dibarten)

They (masc. and fem.)	דיברו(Dibru)

This table demonstrates how the verb "לדבר" (L'daber) is conjugated in the past tense across different subjects in the Pa'al pattern. It provides a clear example of how regular verbs behave in this common Hebrew verb pattern.

Here's a table that covers the patterns פעל (Pa'al), פיעל (Pi'el), הפעיל (Hif'il), נפעל (Nif'al), and התפעל *(Hitpa'el) across different pronouns.*

Conjugation Table for בניינים in Past Tense

Pronoun/Suffix	פעל (Pa'al)	פיעל (Pi'el)	הפעיל (Hif'il)	נפעל (Nif'al)	התפעל (Hitpa'el)
I (תי)	פעלתי (Pa'alti)	פיעלתי (Pi'alti)	הפעלתי (Hif'alti)	נפעלתי (Nif'alti)	התפעלתי (Hitpa'alti)
You (masc.) (ת)	פעלת (Pa'alta)	פיעלת (Pi'alta)	הפעלת (Hif'alta)	נפעלת (Nif'alta)	התפעלת (Hitpa'alta)
You (fem.) (ת)	פעלת (Pa'alt)	פיעלת (Pi'alt)	הפעלת (Hif'alt)	נפעלת (Nif'alt)	התפעלת (Hitpa'alt)
He (ה)	פעל (Pa'al)	פיעל (Pi'el)	הפעיל (Hif'il)	נפעל (Nif'al)	התפעל (Hitpa'el)
She (ה)	פעלה (Pa'alah)	פיעלה (Pi'elah)	הפעילה (Hif'ilah)	נפעלה (Nif'alah)	התפעלה (Hitpa'elah)

We (נו)	פעלנו (Pa'alnu)	פיעלנו (Pi'alnu)	הפעלנו (Hif'alnu)	נפעלנו (Nif'alnu)	התפעלנו (Hitpa'alnu)
You (pl. masc.) (תם)	פעלתם (Pa'alten)	פיעלתם (Pi'alten)	הפעלתם (Hif'alten)	נפעלתם (Nif'altem)	התפעלתם (Hitpa'alten)
You (pl. fem.) (תן)	פעלתן (Pa'alten)	פיעלתן (Pi'alten)	הפעלתן (Hif'alten)	נפעלתן (Nif'alten)	התפעלתן (Hitpa'alten)
They (ו)	פעלו (Pa'alu)	פיעלו (Pi'alu)	הפעילו (Hif'ilu)	נפעלו (Nif'alu)	התפעלו (Hitpa'alu)

This table represents the conjugation of the root ל-ע-פ (P-A-L) in the past tense across different בניינים and pronouns. It's a vital tool for understanding how verbs change according to tense, pattern, and subject in Hebrew.

Past Tense Conjugation Table for בניינים with Roots Ending in ה.י.ו

Creating a conjugation table for the past tense in Hebrew using roots that end with ה.י.ו (H.Y.V) in various בניינים (Binyanim) will help demonstrate how these verbs are modified. Here's a detailed table for the past tense in פעל (Pa'al), פיעל (Pi'el), הפעיל (Hif'il), נפעל (Nif'al), and התפעל (Hitpa'el) using specific verbs that follow this pattern.

- The verb לשחות (Lis'khot) means "to swim," and שחה (Shakha) is its past tense form for "he swam."

- לכסות (Lekhasot) means "to cover," with כסה (Kasa) being "he covered."

- להפרות (Lehafriot) signifies "to separate," and הפרה (Hifra) translates to "he separated."

- להיכבות (Lehikavot) is "to extinguish," with נכבה (Nikva) as "it was extinguished."

- להתרצות (Lehitratzot) means "to justify," and התרצה (Hitratze) is "he justified."

Binyan	(Verb)	(I)	You (m.)	You (f.)	He	She	We	You (pl. m.)	You (pl. f.)	They (m.)	They (f.)
Pa'al	לשחות	שחיתי	שחית	שחית	שחה	שחתה	שחינו	שחיתם	שחיתן	שחו	שחו
Pi'el	לכסות	כיסיתי	כסית	כסית	כסה	כסתה	כסינו	כסיתם	כסיתן	כסו	כסו
Hif'il	להפרות	הפריתי	הפרית	הפרית	הפרה	הפרתה	הפרינו	הפריתם	הפריתן	הפרו	הפרו
Nif'al	להיכבות	נכביתי	נכבית	נכבית	נכבה	נכבתה	נכבינו	נכביתם	נכביתן	נכבו	נכבו
Hitpa'el	להתרצות	התרציתי	התרצית	התרצית	התרצה	התרצתה	התרצינו	התרציתם	התרציתן	התרצו	התרצו

Chapter Summary

This chapter covered the basics of the Hebrew past tense:

- **Understanding Verb Patterns:** You learned about בניינים (Binyanim), the different verb patterns that carry distinct meanings.
- **Past Tense in Action:** You explored how the past tense is formed in Pa'al, Pi'el, Hitpa'el, Nif'al, and Hif'il.
- **Conjugation Patterns:** You learned the common suffixes that indicate the subject of past tense verbs.

Practice

Exercise 1:

In this exercise, you are given a root, a בניין (Binyan), and a pronoun. Your task is to write the correct form of the verb in the past tense. Work through these combinations, and then check your answers with the provided key.

Your Answer	Pronoun	Binyan	Root	No.
	היא	הפעיל	ל.מ.ד	1
	אני	פעל	כ.ת.ב	2
	אנחנו	נפעל	ר.א.ה	3
	הם	פיעל	ש.מ.ע	4
	אתה	התפעל	ד.ב.ר	5
	היא	פעל	ח.ש.ב	6
	אני	הפעיל	ק.נ.ה	7
	הן	פיעל	צ.פ.ה	8
	הוא	התפעל	ב.כ.י	9
	את	נפעל	ג.ל.ה	10

Exercise 2:

Fill in the blanks in each sentence with the correct verb conjugation from the word bank. Remember to change the verb if the pronoun (I, you, he, she, we, they) changes.

Exercise Table:

1. הם _____ (פעל, ה.ל.כ) לסופרמרקט ביחד (They went to the store together.) .

2. היא _____ (פעל, ק.נ.ה) ספר חדש.(She bought a new book.)

3. הם _____ (פעל, א.כ.ל) ארוחת צהריים במסעדה.(They ate lunch at a restaurant.)

4. הם _____ (פעל, ש.ת.ה) קפה אחרי הארוחה.(They drank coffee after the meal.)

5. אני _____ (פעל, ש.ח.ק) כדורגל בפארק.(I played soccer in the park.)

6. היא _____ (פעל, ש.ר) שיר יפה.(She sang a beautiful song.)

7. אנחנו _____ (פעל, ר.ק.ד) כל הלילה.(We danced all night.)

8. את _____ (פעל, ק.ר.א) בעיתון הבוקר?(Did you read the newspaper this morning?)

9. אתה _____ (פעל, ד.ב.ר) איתה בטלפון אתמול. (You spoke with her on the phone yesterday.)

10. אני _____ (פעל, כ.ת.ב) מכתב לחברה שלי.(I wrote a letter to my friend.)

Exercise 3:

לקבל (LeKabel) - to receive

לסדר (LeSader) - to organize

לשחק (LeSaḥek) - to play

לבשל (LeVashel) - to cook

להחליט (Lehaḥlit) - to decide

להסביר (Lehasbir) - to explain

להיפגש (Lehipagesh) - to meet

להיכנס (Lehikanes) - to enter

להישבר (Lehishaver) - to break

#	Root	Binyan	Hebrew Sentence
1	ס.ד.ר	Pi'el	הוא _____ את החדר.
2	פ.ג.ש	Nif'al	_____ חברה אתמול.
3	ש.ב.ר	Pa'al	היא _____ את האגרטל.
4	ס.ב.ר	Hif'il	_____ לו את המצב.
5	ב.ש.ל	Hif'il	הם _____ ארוחת ערב ביחד.
6	ק.ב.ל	Pi'el	היא _____ מתנה ליום ההולדת שלה.
7	כ.נ.ס	Nif'al	_____ לבניין.
8	ש.ח.ק	Pi'el	הם _____ משחקי קופסה.
9	ח.ל.ט	Hif'il	_____ ללמוד עברית.
10	ש.ח.ק	Pi'el	הוא _____ כדורגל עם החברים שלו.

Chapter 1 Answer Key

Exercise 1:

No.	Root	Binyan	Pronoun	Correct Answer
1	ל.מ.ד	הפעיל	היא	הלמידה
2	כ.ת.ב	פעל	אני	כתבתי
3	ר.א.ה	נפעל	אנחנו	נראינו
4	ש.מ.ע	פיעל	הם	שמעו
5	ד.ב.ר	התפעל	אתה	התדברת
6	ח.ש.ב	פעל	היא	חשבה
7	ק.נ.ה	הפעיל	אני	הקניתי
8	צ.פ.ה	פיעל	הן	צפו
9	ב.כ.י	התפעל	הוא	התבכה
10	ג.ל.ה	נפעל	את	נגלית

Exercise 2:

Sentence	Verb	Conjugation	Translation
1	הלכו	פעל, ה.ל.כ	They went

2	קנתה	פעל, ק.נ.ה	She bought
3	אכלו	פעל, א.ב.ל	They ate
4	שתו	פעל, ש.ת.ה	They drank
5	שיחקתי	פעל, ש.ח.ק	I played
6	שרה	פעל, ש.ר	She sang
7	רקדנו	פעל, ר.ק.ד	We danced
8	קראת	פעל, ק.ר.א	Did you (feminine) read?
9	דיברת	פעל, ד.ב.ר	You (masculine) spoke
10	כתבתי	פעל, כ.ת.ב	I wrote

Exercise 3:

No.	Correct Answer
1	סידר
2	נפגשתי
3	שברה
4	הסברתי

5	בישלו
6	קיבלה
7	נכנסנו
8	שיחקו
9	החלטתי
10	שיחק

Coming up...

Explore the different ways to express future tense in Hebrew, including the use of prefixes, suffixes, and root changes, and we will learn how to use the future tense to talk about plans, intentions, and predictions. Let's continue!

Chapter 2 – "What will be, will be"

Where there's a will, there's a way.

אֵין דָּבָר שֶׁעוֹמֵד בִּפְנֵי הָרָצוֹן

In future tense, Hebrew verbs typically use a combination of prefixes and suffixes that vary based on the subject of the verb. Here are the common ones:

Prefixes: Generally, the future tense in Hebrew starts with a prefix (א, ת, י, נ), which corresponds to the subject pronoun.

For example, א (Eh) for I, ת (T) for you, י (Y) for he/she, and נ (N) for we.

The goal of this chapter is to provide you with a comprehensive understanding of forming future tense verbs in various בניינים. By the end, you'll be able to construct sentences about future events and express intentions and plans in Hebrew, thus opening up new dimensions of conversation and expression.

Here's a detailed table for the future tense in the patterns פעל (Pa'al), פיעל (Pi'el), הפעיל (Hif'il), נפעל (Nif'al), and התפעל (Hitpa'el).

Future Tense Conjugation Table for בניינים

Pronoun/Suffix	פעל	פיעל	הפעיל	נפעל	התפעל
I	אפעל	אפעל	אפעיל	איפעל	אתפעל

You (m.)	תפעל / "תפעול"	תפעל	תפעיל	תיפעל	תתפעל
You (f.)	תפעלי	תפעלי	תפעילי	תיפעלי	תתפעלי
He	יפעל	יפעל	יפעיל	ייפעל	יתפעל
She	תפעל	תפעל	תפעיל	תיפעל	תתפעל
We	נפעל	נפעל	נפעיל	ניפעל	נתפעל
You (pl. ma.)	תפעלו	תפעלו	תפעילו	תיפעלו	תתפעלו
You (pl. f.)	תפעלנה	תפעלנה	תפעילנה	תיפעלנה	תתפעלנה
They	יפעלו	יפעלו	יפעילו	ייפעלו	יתפעלו

This table shows the conjugation of the root פ-ע-ל (P-A-L) in the future tense across different בניינים and for various pronouns.

Creating a conjugation table for the future tense in Hebrew with roots ending in ה.י.ו (H.Y.V) across different בניינים illustrates the adaptation of these verbs for future actions or intentions. Here's a detailed table for the future tense in roots that end in ה, י and ו.

Future Tense Conjugation for Roots Ending in ו.י.ה

In this table:

Binyan	Verb	I	You (m.)	You (f.)	He	She	We	You (pl. m.)	You (pl. f.)	They
פעל	לשחות	אשחה	תשחה	תשחי	ישחה	תשחה	נשחה	תשחו	תשחו	ישחו
פיעל	לכסות	אכסה	תכסה	תכסי	יכסה	תכסה	נכסה	תכסו	תכסו	יכסו
הפעיל	להפרות	אפרה	תפרה	תפרי	יפרה	תפרה	נפרה	תפרו	תפרו	יפרו
נפעל	להיכבות	אכבה	תכבה	תכבי	יכבה	תכבה	נכבה	תכבו	תכבו	יכבו
התפעל	להתרצות	אתרצה	תתרצה	תתרצי	יתרצה	תתרצה	נתרצה	תתרצו	תתרצו	יתרצו

- "לשחות" (to swim) follows the Pa'al pattern.

- "לכסות" (to cover) follows the Pi'el pattern.

- "להפרות" (to separate) follows the Hif'il pattern.

- "להיכבות" (to extinguish) follows the Nif'al pattern.

- "להתרצות" (to justify) follows the Hitpa'el pattern.

Chapter Summary

This chapter provided a comprehensive overview of the future tense in Hebrew. By understanding the rules and patterns of future tense conjugation, you will be able to express your intentions and plans in Hebrew! The next chapter will touch exactly on this.

So what is "What will be, will be"?

It is a Hebrew phrase (מה שיהיה יהיה) that is very common in Israeli culture. In the next chapter, we will learn to conjugate it.

Practice

Exercise 1:

Word Bank

- לכתוב
- (Li'khtov) - to write
- לקרוא (Liqro) - to read
- לדבר (L'daber) - to speak
- לאכול (Le'ekhol) - to eat
- לשתות (Li'shtot) - to drink
- לשיר (La'shir) - to sing
- לרקוד (Li'rḳod) - to dance
- לקבל (LeKabel) - to receive
- לסדר (LeSader) - to organize
- לשחק (LeSaḥek) - to play, act
- לבשל (LeVashel) - to cook

- להחליט (Lehaḥlit) - to decide
- להסביר (Lehasbir) - to explain
- להיפגש (Lehipagesh) - to meet
- להיכנס (Lehikanes) - to enter
- להישבר (Lehishaver) - to break
- להתעורר (Lehit'orer) - to wake up
- להתלבש (Lehitlabesh) - to get dressed
- להתפעל (Lehitpa'el) - to be impressed

Exercise Table

#	English Translation	Sentence (with blank)	Root
1	He will organize the room.	הוא _____ את החדר. (Pi'el, Future)	ס.ד.ר

2	I will meet a friend tomorrow.	_____ חברה מחר. (Nif'al, Future)	פ.ג.ש
3	She will break the vase.	היא _____ את האגרטל. (Pa'al, Future)	ש.ב.ר
4	I will explain the situation to him.	_____ לו את המצב. (Hif'il, Future)	ס.ב.ר
5	They will cook dinner together.	הם _____ ארוחת ערב ביחד. (Hif'il, Future)	ב.ש.ל
6	She will receive a present for her birthday.	היא _____ מתנה ליום ההולדת שלה. (Pi'el, Future)	ק.ב.ל
7	We will enter the building.	_____ לבניין. (Nif'al, Future)	כ.נ.ס
8	They will play board games.	הם _____ משחקי קופסה. (Pi'el, Future)	ש.ח.ק
9	I will decide to study Hebrew.	_____ ללמוד עברית. (Hif'il, Future)	ח.ל.ט
10	He will play soccer with his friends.	הוא _____ כדורגל עם החברים שלו. (Pi'el, Future)	ש.ח.ק

Exercise 2:

Sentence (with blank)	#
הם _____ (פעל, ה.ל.כ) לסופרמרקט ביחד.	1
היא _____ (פעל, ק.נ.ה) ספר חדש.	2
הם _____ (פעל, א.כ.ל) ארוחת צהריים במסעדה.	3
הם _____ (פעל, ש.ת.ה) קפה אחרי הארוחה.	4
אני _____ (פעל, ש.ח.ק) כדורגל בפארק.	5
היא _____ (פעל, ש.ר) שיר יפה.	6
אנחנו _____ (פעל, ר.ק.ד) כל הלילה.	7
את _____ (פעל, ק.ר.א) בעיתון הבוקר?	8
אתה _____ (פעל, ד.ב.ר) איתה בטלפון אתמול.	9
אני _____ (פעל, כ.ת.ב) מכתב לחברה שלי.	10

Chapter 2 Answer Key

Exercise 1:

Correct Answer	#
יסדר	1
אפגש	2
תשבור	3
אסביר	4
יבשלו	5
תקבל	6
ניכנס	7
ישחקו	8
אחליט	9
ישחק	10

Exercise 2:

#	Correct Answer
1	ילכו
2	תקנה
3	יאכלו
4	ישתו
5	אשחק
6	תשיר
7	נרקוד
8	תקראי
9	תדבר
10	אכתוב

Coming up...

In the next chapter, we will address hypothetical situations. Or will we? Let's go!

Chapter 3 – Hypotheticals

The journey of a thousand miles begins with a single step.

הַמַּסָּע שֶׁל אָלֶף מִיל מַתְחִיל בְּצַעַד אֶחָד

When we want to express situations that are contrary to facts, imagined possibilities, or wishes in Hebrew, we use hypothetical statements. These sentences let us explore "what if" scenarios, delving into what *could have been* under different circumstances.

The Foundation: The Verb "to be" (להיות)

The cornerstone of hypothetical constructions in Hebrew is the verb "to be" (להיות). Generally, following the verb "to be", we'll find another verb conjugated in the present tense. Let's look at some examples:

- הייתי רוצה לטוס לירח (hayiti rotzeh latus la'yareach) - "I would like to fly to the moon." (expressing a hypothetical wish)

- אם היית עושה את זה, אז כך היה קורה (im hayita oseh et ze, az kach hayah koreh) - "If you had done that, then this would have happened." (Hypothetical cause and effect)

- לו הייתי יודע את זה קודם, הייתי מתנהג אחרת (lu hayiti yodea et ze kodem, hayiti mitnaheg acheret) - "If I had known this before, I would have acted differently." (Regret about a past hypothetical)

Reviewing the Conjugations of להיות *(to be)*

Before diving deeper into hypotheticals, let's solidify our understanding of the verb להיות (to be). This verb is often irregular, so it's helpful to review its conjugation in both the past and future tenses. These forms are essential for constructing different types of hypothetical sentences.

Past Tense

Pronoun	Past Tense (to be)	Example
אני	הייתי (hayiti)	הייתי בבית הספר (hayiti be'vet hasefer) - I was at school
אתה	היית (hayita)	היית עייף (hayita ayef) - You (m) were tired
את	היית (hayit)	היית נחמדה (hayit nehmadah) - You (f) were nice
הוא	היה (hayah)	הוא היה שמח (hu hayah sameach) - He was happy
היא	היתה (hayetah)	היא היתה חולה (hi hayetah cholah) - She was sick
אנחנו	היינו (hayinu)	היינו חברים (hayinu chaverim) - We were friends
אתם	הייתם (hayitem)	הייתם עסוקים (hayitem asukim) - You (m. pl) were busy
אתן	הייתן (hayiten)	הייתן מצחיקות (hayiten metzchikot) - You (f. pl) were funny
הם	היו (hayu)	הם היו רעבים (hem hayu re'evim) - They (m) were hungry

| הן | היו (hayu) | הן היו עייפות (hen hayu ayefot) - They (f) were tired |

Future Tense

Pronoun	Future Tense (to be)	Example
אני	אהיה (ehyeh)	אהיה מאושר (ehyeh me'ushar) - I will be happy
אתה	תהיה (tihyeh)	בסדר תהיה (tihyeh beseder) - You (m) will be okay
את	תהיי (tihyi)	חזקה תהיי (tihyi chazakah) - You (f) will be strong
הוא	יהיה (yihyeh)	כיף יהיה (yihyeh kef) - It will be fun (m)
היא	תהיה (tihyeh)	יפה תהיה (tihyeh yafah) - She will be beautiful
אנחנו	נהיה (nihyeh)	יחד נהיה (nihyeh yachad) - We will be together
אתם	תהיו (tihyu)	בריאים תהיו (tihyu bri'im) - You (m. pl) will be healthy
אתן	תהיו (tihyen)	שמחות תהיו (tihyen smechot) - You (f. pl) will be happy

הם	יהיו (yihyu)	עצובים יהיו (yihyu atzuvim) - They (m) will be sad
הן	יהיו (yihyu)	עייפות יהיו (yihyu ayefot) - They (f) will be tired

Types of Hypotheticals

Hebrew offers flexibility with hypotheticals, covering different scenarios:

- **Heartfelt Wishes:** אני מצטער שאני לא יכול להיות שם. הייתי רוצה להיות איתך (ani mitsta'er she'ani lo yachol lihyot sham. hayiti rotzeh lihyot itach.) - "I'm sorry I can't be there. I wish I could be with you."

- **Impossible Conditions in the Present:** אם היית פה עכשיו, היינו הולכים יחד לים (im hayita po achshav, hayinu holchim yachad la'yam) - "If you were here now, we would go to the sea together."

- **Past Regrets:** לו הייתי יודעת מה שאני יודעת היום, הייתי עושה דברים אחרת (lu hayiti yoda'at ma she'ani yoda'at hayom, hayiti osah dvarim acheret) - "If only I had known then what I know now, I would have done things differently."

Syntax Breakdown: Hypotheticals Expressing Wishes

The basic building blocks of these sentences are:

- הייתי רוצה **(hayiti rotzeh/rotzah)** - This phrase literally translates to "I would have wanted." The gender of the speaker determines whether you use רוצה or רוצה.

- **Verb in the Infinitive Form** - This follows directly after "הייתי רוצה" and indicates the action or state you wish for.

Examples:

- הייתי רוצה לטוס לירח (hayiti rotzeh latus la'yareach) - "I would like to fly to the moon."

- הייתי רוצה לאכול עוגה (hayiti rotzah le'echol uga) - "I would like to eat cake."

- הייתי רוצה להיות איתך (hayiti rotzeh lihyot itach) - "I wish I could be with you."

Even though the phrase "הייתי רוצה" seems to refer to the past, it actually sets up a wish in the present. It's a way to express a desire politely. The structure is relatively fixed in Hebrew. Stress the importance of keeping "הייתי רוצה" followed immediately by

Here's a breakdown of the syntax and examples for impossible conditions in the present tense in Hebrew:

Syntax: Impossible Conditions in the Present

The key elements needed to construct these sentences are:

- אם **(im)** - This word means "if".

- היית / הייתם / הייתן / היית / היו **(hayita/ hayitem/ hayiten/ hayit/ hayu)** - Conjugations of the verb "to be" (להיות) in the past tense. Choose the conjugation based on the subject of the sentence (who or what is doing the hypothetical action).
- **Verb in the Present Tense** - The verb following the conjugation of "to be" expresses the hypothetical action.

Important Note: Even though we're using the past tense of "to be", this structure expresses an impossible condition **in the present**. We use this form to emphasize the contrast between the wish and the reality.

Examples:

- אם היית פה עכשיו, הייתי נותן לך חיבוק גדול (im hayita po achshav, hayiti noten lecha chibuk gadol) - "If you were here now, I would give you a big hug."

- אם היו לי כנפיים, הייתי עפה לשמיים (im hayu li knafayim, hayiti afa la'shamayim) - "If I had wings, I would fly to the heavens."

- אם הייתם יודעים את התשובה, הייתם אומרים לי (im hayitem yoda'im et ha'teshuva, hayitem omrim li) - "If you knew the answer, you would tell me."

Key Points to Emphasize:

- **Impossibility:** Stress that the conditions described in these sentences cannot be true in the present moment, making them hypothetical.

- **Implication:** Even though the focus is on the present, this construction often implies a consequence of the condition being true. For example, *"If you were here, I would give you a big hug"* suggests that, because you're not here, the hug isn't happening.

Syntax: Hypotheticals Expressing Regret

The structure for these sentences typically includes:

- לו **(lu)** - This word means "if only" or "if I had..."

- היו / היית / הייתן / הייתם / הייתי **(hayiti/ hayitem/ hayiten/ hayit/ hayu)** - Conjugations of the verb "to be" (להיות) in the past tense. Match the conjugation to the subject of your hypothetical situation.

- **Verb in the Past Tense** - This verb expresses the action or state that you cannot change or regret not having done.

The Importance of Past Tense: Using both the past tense of "to be" and a past tense verb is crucial to conveying a sense of regret about a situation in the past that can't be altered.

Examples:

- לו הייתי רוטשילד, הייתי קונה אי (lu hayiti Rothschild, hayiti koneh i) - "If only I were a Rothschild, I would buy an island."

- לו הייתם אומרים לי את זה קודם, לא הייתי טועה (lu hayitem omrim li et ze kodem, lo hayiti to'eh) - " If you had told me that earlier, I wouldn't have made a mistake."

- לו הייתי יודעת כמה זה כיף, הייתי מתחילה קודם (lu hayiti yoda'at kama ze kef, hayiti matchilah kodem) - "If I had known how fun this was, I would have started earlier."

Beyond "lu": Note that there are other words in Hebrew that can introduce hypothetical situations, such as אלמלא (ilmalei).

Chapter Summary

- **The Power of** להיות**:** The verb להיות (to be) is the foundation for constructing most hypothetical statements in Hebrew.
- **Hypothetical Types**
  - **Wishes in the present:** We use "הייתי רוצה" + [verb in infinitive] to talk about desires like "I would like to..."
  - **Impossible conditions in the present:** We use "אם" + [past tense of להיות] + [verb in present] to express things like "If I had..., I would..."
  - **Past regrets:** We use "לו" + [past tense of להיות] + [verb in past tense] to convey regret about past events, such as "If only I had known..., I would have..."
- **Beyond the Basics:** We hinted that other words like אלמלא (ilmalei) also function in hypothetical situations.
- **Verb Review:** We reviewed the past and future tense conjugations of the verb להיות (to be), which are essential for building complex hypotheticals.

Practice

Exercise 1:

Instructions: Read each sentence carefully. In the "Hypothetical?" column, write "Yes" if the sentence is a hypothetical statement and "No" if it is not. If it *is* hypothetical, identify the type.

Type	Hypothetical?	Sentence (Hebrew)
		אני הולכת לבית הספר.
		מחר תהיה מסיבה.
		אם הייתי יודעת את זה, הייתי עוזרת.
		אנחנו אוכלים פסטה לארוחת ערב.
		הייתי רוצה לנסוע לתאילנד.
		לו היה לי הרבה כסף, הייתי נוסע מסביב לעולם.
		לו הייתם מקשיבים לי, לא הייתם עושים את הטעות הזאת.
		השמש זורחת היום.
		אם היה לי יותר זמן פנוי, הייתי לומד לנגן בגיטרה.

		אולי נלך לים מחר.	

Exercise 2:

Instructions: Complete each hypothetical sentence by choosing the correct words and verb forms from the word bank. Pay close attention to verb conjugations, sentence structure, and the type of hypothetical situation expressed.

Word Bank: אם, הייתי, היית, היינו, היה, היינו, לו, נוסעת, נוסעים, נוסע, עוזר, עוזרת, מדברים, מדברות, קונה, קונים, יש, אוכלים, אוכלים

Word 2	Word 1	Incomplete Sentence (Hebrew)	#
		... לך מתנה אם ... לי יותר כסף.	1
		... איתכם אם לא ... צריכים לעבוד.	2
		... איתי אמש אם ... מזמינה/מזמין אותך.	3
		לו... עכשיו קיץ, ... הולכים לים.	4
		לא ... כל כך עצובה/עצוב לו ... איתי החתול/החתולה שלי.	5
		... עכשיו בפריז אם ... כרטיס טיסה.	6

		לו ... את כל התשובות, ... מקבל/מקבלת 100 במבחן.	7
		... עכשיו במסעדה טובה אם ... לנו הזמנה.	8
		... לי את האמת אם ... שואל/שואלת אותך.	9
		כל החלומות שלי ... מתגשמים אם ... לי שרביט קסמים.	10

Chapter 3 Answer Key

Exercise 1:

Type	Hypothetical?	Sentence (Hebrew)
	No	אני הולכת לבית הספר.
	No	מחר תהיה מסיבה.
Past Regret	Yes	אם הייתי יודעת את זה, הייתי עוזרת.
	No	אנחנו אוכלים פסטה לארוחת ערב.
Wish	Yes	הייתי רוצה לנסוע לתאילנד.
Impossible Condition	Yes	לו היה לי הרבה כסף, הייתי נוסע מסביב לעולם.
Past Regret	Yes	לו הייתם מקשיבים לי, לא הייתם עושים את הטעות הזאת.
	No	השמש זורחת היום.
Impossible Condition	Yes	אם היה לי יותר זמן פנוי, הייתי לומד לנגן בגיטרה.
	No	אולי נלך לים מחר.

Exercise 2:

Potential Answer 2	Potential Answer 1	#
היה	הייתי קונה	1
היינו	היינו באים	2
הייתי	היית באה	3
היינו	היה	4
היה	הייתי	5
היה	הייתי נוסעת	6
הייתי	הייתי יודעת	7
הייתה	היינו אוכלים	8
הייתי	היית מספרת	9
היה	היו	10

Coming up...

In the next chapter, we will learn how to "get around" in Israel, practice speaking with tax drivers (for example), and explore conversational etiquette in Israel. Let's go!

Chapter 4 – Getting Around

Mistakes are the doorways to discovery.

הַטָּעֻיּוֹת הֵן הַפְּתָחִים לְגִלּוּיִים

Getting around a foreign country can be intimidating, especially when you don't speak the language. Israel is no different. This chapter will give you the key Hebrew words and phrases you need to navigate common travel situations in Israel with more confidence.

We'll focus on three main scenarios you're likely to encounter during your travels:

- **Hailing a Taxi (לתפוס מונית):** Learn how to ask for directions, give your destination, and understand basic fare questions.
- **Checking into a Hotel (צ'ק אין למלון):** Practice making reservations, asking about amenities, and handling any potential issues that might arise.
- **Shopping (קניות):** Discover the words you'll need for browsing in stores, asking for prices, and making purchases.

Key Vocabulary

Throughout the chapter, we'll introduce words like:

- Yes (כן)
- No (לא)
- Sorry (סליחה)
- Please (בבקשה)
- Maybe (אולי)
- Need (צריך/צריכה)

- Want (רוצה/רוצה)

- Speak (מדבר/מדברת)

- Don't speak (לא מדבר/לא מדברת)

Taxis

When traveling in Israel, taxis offer a convenient way to get around cities. Here's what you need to know about finding and communicating with taxi drivers in Hebrew:

Key Vocabulary

- **Taxi:** מונית ("moh-neet")

- **Where to?** לאן? ("leh-ahn")

- **Please take me to...** ...בבקשה קח/קחי אותי ל ("bevakasha kach/kachi oti le...")

- **Stop here, please** תעצור/תעצרי כאן בבקשה ("ta'atzor/ta'atzri kan bevakasha")

- **How much?** כמה זה? ("kamah zeh?")

- **Meter** מונה ("moneh")

- **Turn on the meter, please** בבקשה תפעיל/תפעלי מונה ("bevakasha taf'il/taf'ili moneh")

Scenario 1:

- You: סליחה! מונית! (Excuse me! Taxi!)

- Taxi Driver: לאן? (Where to?)

- You: בבשה תיקח אותי לבית מלון דן, בבקשה. (Please take me to the Dan Hotel.)

- Taxi Driver: בסדר. (Okay.)

Scenario 2:

- You: שלום, אני רוצה להזמין מונית לבית מלון הילטון, בבקשה. (Hello, I'd like to order a taxi to the Hilton Hotel, please.)

- Taxi Dispatcher: מאיפה? (From where?)

- You: מרחוב הירקון 20. (From 20 Hayarkon Street.)

- Taxi Dispatcher: עוד כמה דקות המונית תגיע. (The taxi will arrive in a few minutes.)

Checking into a Hotel

- Hotel: מלון ("mah-lohn")

- Reservation: הזמנה ("haz-ma-nah")

- Room: חדר ("cheh-der")

- Single room: חדר יחיד ("cheh-der ya-chid")

- Double room: חדר זוגי ("cheh-der zu-gi")

- Night: לילה ("lay-lah")

- Breakfast: ארוחת בוקר ("aru-chat boh-ker")

- Included: כלול ("ka-lul")

- Passport: דרכון ("dar-kon")

Scenario 1:

- You: שלום, יש לי הזמנה על שם... (Hello, I have a reservation under the name...)

- Receptionist: כן, בבקשה את הדרכון שלך. (Yes, please provide your passport.)

- You: הנה. (Here it is.)

- Receptionist: חדר זוגי לשני לילות, ארוחת בוקר כלולה. (A double room for two nights, breakfast included.)
- You: מצוין, תודה. (Excellent, thank you.)

Scenario 2:

- You: שלום, יש לכם חדר פנוי להלילה? (Hello, do you have a room available for tonight?)
- Receptionist: איזה סוג חדר? (What type of room?)
- You: חדר יחיד, בבקשה. (A single room, please.)
- Receptionist: כן, יש לנו. זה יעלה 500 שקל ללילה. (Yes, we do. It will cost 500 shekels per night.)
- You: בסדר, אני רוצה את זה. (Okay, I'll take it.)

Important Questions

- האם ארוחת בוקר כלולה? (Is breakfast included?)
- באיזו שעה הצ'ק אאוט? (What time is check-out?)
- יש אינטרנט אלחוטי בחדר? (Is there Wi-Fi in the room?)
- איפה המעלית? (Where is the elevator?)

Shopping in Israel (קניות)

- Store: חנות ("cha-noot")
- Market: שוק ("shuk")
- I'm looking for...: ...אני מחפש/מחפשת ("ani me-chap-es/me-chap-set")
- How much does this cost?: כמה זה עולה? ("ka-ma zeh o-leh?")
- That's too expensive: זה יקר מדי ("zeh ya-kar mi-dai")

- Do you have this in a different color/size?: יש לך את זה בצבע/מידה אחר/ת? ("yesh lecha et zeh be-tzeva/mi-dah acher/acheret?")

- I'd like to buy this: אני רוצה לקנות את זה ("ani rotzeh/rotzah liknot et zeh")

- Can I try this on?: אני יכול/יכולה למדוד את זה? ("ani yachol/yecholah limdod et zeh?")

- I'll take it: אני אקח את זה ("ani ekach et zeh")

Scenario 1:

- You: שלום, אני מחפשת שמלה. (Hello, I'm looking for a dress.)

- Salesperson: איזה סוג שמלה? לאירוע? (What kind of dress? For an event?)

- You: משהו קליל ליום יום. (Something casual for everyday wear.)

- Salesperson: יש לנו כמה שמלות נחמדות פה. את יכולה למדוד. (We have some nice dresses here. You can try them on.)

- You: (After trying on a dress) אני אוהבת את זה! כמה זה עולה? (I like this one! How much is it?)

- Salesperson: 200 שקל. (200 shekels.)

- You: אני אקח את זה. (I'll take it.)

Scenario 2:

- You: כמה עולה קילו עגבניות? (How much is a kilo of tomatoes?)

- Vendor: 10 שקל לקילו. (10 shekels per kilo.)

- You: זה יקר מדי. יש לך מחיר יותר טוב? (That's too expensive. Do you have a better price?)

- Vendor: בשבילך, 8 שקל לקילו. (For you, 8 shekels a kilo.)

- You: בסדר גמור, אני אקח שני קילו. (Okay, great. I'll take two kilos.)

Scenario 3:

- You: אני מחפש מתנה לחבר. (I'm looking for a gift for a friend.)

- Shopkeeper: מה הוא אוהב? (What does he like?)

- You: הוא אוהב דברים שקשורים לישראל. (He likes things related to Israel.)

- Shopkeeper: יש לנו חמסות יפות מעץ זית. (We have beautiful olive wood hamsas.)

- You: זה רעיון טוב! יש לך את זה בצבע אחר? (That's a good idea! Do you have it in another color?)

- Shopkeeper: כן, יש גם בכחול. (Yes, we also have it in blue.)

- You: אני אקח את הכחולה. (I'll take the blue one.)

Chapter Summary

In this chapter, we've equipped you with some Hebrew vocabulary and phrases to handle common travel situations in Israel:

- Learning to ask for directions, give your destination, understand fares, and request the meter to be turned on.
- Practicing making reservations, asking about amenities, and understanding the check-in process.
- Mastering how to ask for items, inquire about prices, try things on, negotiate, and make purchases in stores and markets.

Practice

Exercise 1:

Hailing a Taxi

Practice Exercise

Instructions: Complete the sentences below about hailing a taxi in Israel. Choose the correct words from the word bank and conjugate the verbs appropriately.

1. _____! אני צריך/צריכה ללכת לתחנה המרכזית.

2. נהג המונית שואל אותך? _____ :

3. את אומרת _____ :אותי למלון כרמל. _____ ,

4. את רוצה שהנהג ידליק את המונה. את אומרת. _____ _____ , _____ :

5. הגעת למלון. את אומרת לנהג. _____ , _____ _____ :

6. את רוצה לשלם. את שואלת את הנהג _____ :זה?

Exercise 2:

Checking into a Hotel

Word Bank

- יש (there is)

- לי (to me / for me)

- הזמנה (reservation)

- על שם (under the name of)

- כולל (includes)

- ארוחת בוקר (breakfast)

- דרכון (passport)

- בבקשה (please)

- לילות (nights)
- חדר זוגי (double room)
- חדר יחיד (single room)
- לא (no)

Complete the sentences below about checking into a hotel in Israel. Choose the correct words from the word bank and adjust them as needed to fit the sentences.

1. שלום, _____ _____ _____ הזמנה _____ [.Your Name]

2. פקידת הקבלה אומרת: כן, _____ הדרכון שלך.

3. את אומרת: הזמנתי _____ _____ _____ לשלושה _____.

4. פקידת הקבלה: _____ לנו חדרים פנויים מסוג זה.

5. את שואלת: אולי יש חדר _____ במקום?

6. פקידת הקבלה: כן, יש חדר _____ פנוי.

7. את שואלת: ארוחת בוקר _____ במחיר?

8. פקידת הקבלה אומרת: כן, ארוחת בוקר _____.

Exercise 3:

Word Bank

- אני מחפש/מחפשת (I'm looking for - masc./fem.)
- יש (there is/do you have)
- לך/לכם (to you - singular/plural)
- את זה (this - object)
- בצבע (in the color)
- אחר/אחרת (another - masc./fem.)

- מידה (size)
- יותר (more)
- גדול/גדולה (big - masc./fem.)
- קטן/קטנה (small - masc./fem.)
- למדוד (to try on)
- אפשר (possible)
- כמה (how much)

- זה עולה (this costs)

Complete the sentences below about shopping in Israel. Choose the correct words from the word bank and adjust them as needed to fit the sentences.

Scenario 1: Clothing Store

1. שלום, _____ _____ חולצה לגבר.

2. המוכר/ת שואל/ת: _____ _____ חולצה בצבע כחול?

3. כן, אבל אני רוצה _____ בצבע אדום.

4. המוכר/ת: רגע, אני אבדוק. כן, _____ חולצה אדומה במידה _____ .

5. תודה! _____ _____ אותה?

Scenario 2: Market

6. שלום, _____ _____ ענבים?

7. המוכר: כן, יש ענבים טריים ומתוקים!

8. _____ זה עולה לקילו?

9. המוכר: 20 שקל לקילו.

10. יקר! אפשר לקבל מחיר _____ טוב?

Scenario 3: Souvenir Shop

11. אני _____ _____ מתנה לאחותי.

12. המוכר/ת: מה היא אוהבת?

13. היא אוהבת תכשיטים. _____ _____ שרשרת יפה?

14. כן, יש לנו שרשראות כסף בעבודת יד. _____ _____ _____ שרשרת _____?

Chapter 4 Answer Key

Exercise 1:

Answer	#
מונית	1
לאן	2
בבקה	3
בבקשה	4
תעצור/תעצרי	5
כמה	6

Exercise 2:

Answer	#
יש	1
בבקשה	2
חדר זוגי	3

לא	4
יחיד	5
יחיד	6
כולל	7
כלולה	8

Exercise 3:

Answer	#
אני מחפש	1
יש	2
את זה	3
יש	4
אפשר	5
יש	6
כן	7
כמה	8

Coming up...

In the next chapter, we will continue to apply what we have learned in the above chapters to talk about time, namely, how time is handled in Israel.

Chapter 5 – A Time to Celebrate

I did my best, and that's all that matters.

עָשִׂיתִי אֶת הַטוֹב שֶׁיָּכֹלְתִּי, וְזֶה כָּל מַה שֶׁחָשׁוּב

Understanding how to talk about time is critical for navigating daily life in any country. In Israel, time is marked not only by the standard calendar but also by the rhythm of the Jewish holidays, the changing seasons, and even popular sports.

Knowing how to talk about time in Hebrew will help you coordinate your trip around the holidays or choose the perfect season to visit based on your preferences. You can deepen your understanding of Israeli culture by learning about the significance of Jewish holidays and traditions. And you can engage in everyday discussions about the weather, upcoming events, or even your favourite sports team!

Jewish Holidays in Israel

Important Holidays

- **Rosh Hashanah (ראש השנה):** The Jewish New Year, a time of reflection and celebration.

- **Yom Kippur (יום כיפור):** The Day of Atonement, a solemn day of fasting and prayer.

- **Sukkot (סוכות):** A week-long harvest festival where families dwell in temporary huts (Sukkah).

- **Hanukkah (חנוכה):** The eight-day festival of lights, commemorating the rededication of the Temple.

- **Purim (פורים):** A joyous festival celebrating the story of Queen Esther, often marked with costumes and carnivals.

- **Passover (פסח):** Commemorates the Exodus from Egypt, observed with a special Seder meal and the week-long avoidance of leavened bread.

Rosh Hashanah:

- שנה טובה (Shanah Tovah) - "Happy New Year"

- תפוח בדבש (Apple dipped in honey) - Symbolizes wishes for a sweet new year

- שופר (Shofar) - Ram's horn, traditionally blown during services

Sukkot:

- סוכה (Sukkah) - Temporary hut

- ארבעת המינים (Arba'at Haminim) - The four species (lulav, etrog, hadas, aravah)

Hanukkah:

- חנוכיה (Hanukkiah) - Eight-branched candelabra

- סביבון (Dreidel) - Spinning top

- דמי חנוכה (Hanukkah Gelt) - Chocolate coins

Scenario 1:

- Person A: מה התוכניות שלך לראש השנה? (What are your plans for Rosh Hashanah?)

- Person B: אני נוסע/נוסעת להורים שלי לחג. (I'm going to my parents for the holiday.)

- Person A: שנה טובה! (Happy New Year!)

Scenario 2:

- Person A: מה זה סוכה? (What is a Sukkah?)

- Person B: סוכה היא מבנה ארעי שאוכלים בה וישנים בה במהלך חג הסוכות. (A Sukkah is a temporary structure where we eat and sleep during the holiday of Sukkot.)

Seasons in Israel

- חורף (Khoref): Winter (December - February)

- אביב (Aviv): Spring (March - May)

- קיץ (Kayitz): Summer (June - August)

- סתיו (Stav): Autumn (September - November)

Vocabulary Word Bank: Seasons

- קר (Kar): Cold

- חם (Cham): Hot

- גשום (Gashum): Rainy

- נעים (Na'im): Pleasant

- לח (Lach): Humid

Months of the Jewish Calendar

- תשרי (Tishrei): Corresponds roughly to September/October

- חשוון (Cheshvan): Corresponds roughly to October/November

- כסלו (Kislev): Corresponds roughly to November/December

- טבת (Tevet): Corresponds roughly to December/January

- שבט (Shevat): Corresponds roughly to January/February

- אדר (Adar): Corresponds roughly to February/March

- ניסן (Nissan): Corresponds roughly to March/April

- אייר (Iyar): Corresponds roughly to April/May

- סיוון (Sivan): Corresponds roughly to May/June

- תמוז (Tammuz): Corresponds roughly to June/July

- אב (Av): Corresponds roughly to July/August

- אלול (Elul): Corresponds roughly to August/September

Short Story Using the Vocabulary

הגיע חודש תשרי, והימים מתקצרים. בחוץ כבר קצת קר, ומתחילים לרדת גשמים ראשונים של החורף. בשוק, מריחים את הרימונים הטריים והתפוחים המתוקים - סימנים של הסתיו. בקרוב יגיע ראש השנה, ואחר כך חג הסוכות עם הסוכה במרפסת. איזה כיף שהאביב יגיע במהרה, עם מזג אוויר נעים וטיולים בפריחה!

The month of Tishrei has arrived, and the days are getting shorter. It's already a bit cold outside, and the first rains of winter are beginning to fall. In the market, you smell fresh pomegranates and sweet apples – signs of autumn. Soon, Rosh Hashanah will arrive, and afterward, the holiday of Sukkot will begin with the sukkah on the balcony. How nice it will be when spring (Aviv) arrives soon, with pleasant weather and blooming flowers for hikes!

Sports Talk in Israel

Israelis are passionate about sports, with football (soccer) and basketball reigning supreme. Whether you're cheering on your favourite team or discussing the latest match, here's the vocabulary you need to join the conversation.

Popular Sports

- כדורגל (Kaduregel): Football (Soccer)

- כדורסל (Kadursal): Basketball

- טניס (Tennis)

- שחייה (Schiya): Swimming

Key Verbs

- לשחק (Lesachek): To play

- לנצח (Lenatzeach): To win

- להפסיד (Lehafsid): To lose

- לאהוד (Le'ehod): To support/cheer for

- לצפות (Litzpot): To watch

Vocabulary Word Banks

Football (Soccer)

- קבוצה (Kvutza): Team

- שחקן/שחקנית (Sachkan/Sachkanit): Player

- שוער (Sho'er): Goalkeeper

- משחק (Mischak): Game/Match

- בעיטה (Be'ita): Kick

- גול (Goal): Goal

Basketball

- סל (Sal): Basket

- כדור (Kadur): Ball

- לזרוק (Lizrok): To throw

- לקלוע (Likloa): To score (a basket)

- ליגת העל (Ligat Ha'al): Israeli Premier Basketball League

Example Conversations

Scenario 1: Discussing a Football Match

- Person A: ראית את המשחק אתמול? (Did you see the game yesterday?)

- Person B: כן! איזה משחק מדהים! בית"ר ירושלים ניצחו 1-3. (Yes! What an amazing game! Beitar Jerusalem won 3-1.)

Scenario 2: Talking About Favorite Sports

- Person A: מה הספורט האהוב עליך? (What's your favorite sport?)

- Person B: אני אוהב/ת כדורסל. אני אוהד/ת של מכבי תל אביב. (I love basketball. I'm a fan of Maccabi Tel Aviv.)

Short Story

איתי וחבריו התכוננו לערב גדול. המשחק בין מכבי חיפה למכבי תל אביב עמד להתחיל, והאווירה הייתה מתוחה. איתי צעק "גול!" בכל פעם שמכבי חיפה קלעה סל. בסוף המשחק, מכבי תל אביב הפסידו, ואיתי היה מאוכזב. אבל הוא כבר התרגש למשחק הבא!

Itai and his friends were getting ready for a big night. The game between Maccabi Haifa and Maccabi Tel Aviv was about to start, and the atmosphere was tense. Itai shouted "Goal!" every time Maccabi Haifa scored a basket. At the end of the game, Maccabi Tel Aviv lost, and Itai was disappointed. But he was already excited for the next match!

Chapter Summary

This chapter equipped you with the Hebrew vocabulary you need to discuss time, holidays, seasons, and sports in Israel. We covered:

- We explored the names, significance, and key vocabulary of major holidays like Rosh Hashanah, Yom Kippur, Sukkot, Hanukkah, Purim, and Passover.
- You learned the Hebrew words for seasons (summer, winter, etc.) and the months of the Jewish calendar.
- We delved into the lingo of popular sports like football (soccer) and basketball.

Practice

Exercise 1:

Word Bank

- תשרי / Tishrei - The Jewish month roughly corresponding to Sept/Oct

- חם / Cham - Hot

- ראש השנה / Rosh Hashanah - Jewish New Year

- סליחה / Slicha - Sorry

- לשחק / Lesachek - To play

- כדורגל / Kaduregel - Football (soccer)

- חברים / Chaverim - Friends

- אחר הצהריים / Achar Hatzahara'im - Afternoon

- גשם / Geshem - Rain

- אביב / Aviv - Spring

Short Story

בתשרי, הימים היו עדיין חמים, אבל מתן כבר הרגיש את ראש השנה מתקרב. "סליחה!" הוא צעק לחברים שלו במגרש הכדורגל, "אני צריך ללכת הביתה להתכונן לחג". אחר הצהריים התחיל לרדת גשם קל, ומתן חשב כמה יהיה נעים לטייל בפריחה כשיגיע האביב.

Questions

1. באיזה חודש מתרחש הסיפור? (In which month does the story take place?)

2. איך היה מזג האוויר? (How was the weather?)

3. ‏למה מתן היה צריך לעזוב את המשחק?‏ (Why did Matan have to leave the game?)

4. ‏על איזה עונה מתן חשב?‏ (Which season was Matan thinking about?)

Exercise 2:

Here's a longer exercise with a new story, vocabulary, and diverse grammar questions:

Word Bank

- ‏סוכות‏ / Sukkot - The harvest festival of booths

- ‏סוכה‏ / Sukkah - Temporary hut

- ‏לקשט‏ / Lekashet - To decorate

- ‏ישן‏ / Yashen - Sleeps

- ‏קר‏ / Kar - Cold

- ‏סתיו‏ / Stav - Autumn

- ‏חשוון‏ / Cheshvan - Jewish month roughly corresponding to Oct/Nov

- ‏כדורסל‏ / Kadursal - Basketball

- ‏משחק‏ / Mischak - Game

- ‏טלוויזיה‏ / Televizia - Television

Story

‏אחרי ראש השנה, הגיע חג הסוכות. דני ומשפחתו עבדו קשה כדי לקשט את הסוכה שלהם. הם‏
‏תלו קישוטים צבעוניים, פירות וירקות, ושרשראות מנייר. בלילה, דני ישן בסוכה. היה קצת קר,‏
‏אבל הוא התכרבל בשמיכה וחלם על כל המשחקים שישחק בסוכות עם חברים. אחר כך, בחודש‏

חשוון, הימים בסתיו כבר התקצרו. דני אהב לצפות במשחקי כדורסל בטלוויזיה ולדמיין שהוא אחד

השחקנים על המגרש.

Questions

1. איזה חג חגגה משפחתו של דני בתחילת הסיפור? (What holiday did Dani's family celebrate at the beginning of the story?)

2. איך הם קישטו את הבית שלהם? (How did they decorate their house?)

3. איפה דני ישן במהלך החג? (Where did Dani sleep during the holiday?)

4. תאר/י את מזג האוויר בחודש חשוון. (Describe the weather in the month of Cheshvan.)

5. מה דני אהב לעשות בסתיו? (What did Dani like to do in the autumn?)

Chapter 5 Answer Key

Exercise 1:

Answer	#
תשרי	1
חם, עם גשם קל אחר הצהריים	2
הוא היה צריך להתכונן לראש השנה	3
אביב	4

Exercise 2:

Answer	#
סוכות	1
הם תלו קישוטים, פירות, ירקות, ושרשראות	2
בסוכה	3
הימים התקצרו, היה קר	4
לצפות בכדורסל בטלוויזיה	5

Coming up...

In the next chapter, we will cover more basic conversational skills, as well as learn about the core features of the makeup of Hebrew and its origins in Biblical Hebrew (and this includes rules about advanced possession, something still used today!).

Chapter 6 – Next Steps

Learn from yesterday, live for today, hope for tomorrow.

תִּלְמַד מִן הָאֶתְמוֹל ,חֲיֵה לְמַעַן הַיּוֹם ,קַוֵּה לְמַעַן הַמָּחָר

You've mastered the basics of Hebrew, but you're hungry for more! In this chapter, we'll take your skills to the next level and unlock a richer understanding of the language.

We will touch on how to express ownership like a pro with possessive suffixes (בֵּיתָם ,שׁוּלחָנך, etc.). No more awkward workarounds; you'll be speaking with precision. We will get a taste of Biblical Hebrew with common phrases like "וַיֹּאמֶר" (and He said) and "וַיְהִי" (and it was so). This will deepen your connection with the ancient roots of the language. In addition, we will practice some basic conversational skills for different situations, such as blind dates.

Mastering Advanced Possession

In basic Hebrew, we express "of" using the word שֶׁל (shel). But Hebrew has a more elegant way – possessive suffixes! These attach directly to nouns, showing who owns something.

Key Suffixes

Suffix	Meaning	Example Word	Example Translation
ִי-	my	שֻׁלְחָנִי (shulchani)	my table
ךָ-	your (masculine singular)	כִּסְאֲךָ (kis'acha)	your chair
ךְ-	your (feminine singular)	סִפְרֵךְ (sifrech)	your book

ו -	his	בֵּיתוֹ (beito)	his house
ה -	her	מִטָּתָה (mitatah)	her bed
נוּ -	our	כִּתָּתֵנוּ (kitatenu)	our class
כֶם-	your (masculine plural)	סִפְרֵיכֶם (sifreichem)	your books
כֶן-	your (feminine plural)	מִטּוֹתֵיכֶן (mitoteichen)	your beds
ם -	their (masculine)	כְּלְבָּם (kilbam)	their dog
ן -	their (feminine)	חֲנוּתָן (chanutan)	their store

Biblical Hebrew tends to look extremely similar to modern Hebrew, while there are many caveats as well. Let's take a glance at some common Biblical Hebrew grammatical structures:

- ויאמר **(Vayomer):** "And he said..."

- ויהי **(Vayehi):** "And it was so..." or "And it came to pass..."

- ויאהב **(Vayahav):** "And he loved..."

- ותאמר **(Vatomer):** "And she said..."

- וירא **(Vayira):** "And he saw..."

Example Sentences

- ויאמר משה אל העם: "אל תיראו!" (And Moses said to the people: "Do not fear!")

- ויהי אור (And there was light)

- ויאהב יעקב את רחל (And Jacob loved Rachel)

Situational Practice

Blind dates can be exciting but also nerve-wracking, especially in another language. Here's the Hebrew vocabulary and phrases you need to make a great impression:

Word Bank

- דייט עיוור או שידוך / Date Iver - Blind Date

- להכיר / Lehakir - To meet (someone new), get to know

- נעים מאוד / Na'im Me'od - Nice to meet you

- רווק/רווקה / Ravak/Ravakah - Single (man/woman)

- ?בן/בת כמה את/ה / Ben/Bat Kama At/Ata? - How old are you?

- ?מה את/ה עושה / Ma At/Ata Oseh/Osah? - What do you do? (occupation)

- מעניין / Me'anyen - Interesting

- מצחיק/מצחיקה / Matzchik/Matzchikah - Funny

- יש לך עיניים יפות / Yesh Lach Eynayim Yafot - You have beautiful eyes

Short Story

שרה התכוננה לדייט עיוור הראשון שלה. היא הייתה קצת לחוצה אבל גם מתרגשת להכיר מישהו חדש. במסעדה, היא פגשה את ירון. "נעים מאוד," היא אמרה בחיוך. הם התחילו לדבר. ירון סיפר שהוא רווק ועובד כמהנדס. שרה שאלה אותו: "בן כמה אתה?" הם דיברו על תחביבים, סיפרו בדיחות, וצחקו הרבה. שרה חשבה שירון היה גם חכם וגם מצחיק. בסוף הערב, היא אמרה לו, "יש לך עיניים יפות".

Sarah was getting ready for her first blind date. She was a little nervous but also excited to meet someone new. At the restaurant, she met Yaron. "Nice to meet you," she said with a smile. They started talking. Yaron told her that he was single and worked as an engineer. Sarah asked him,

"How old are you?" They talked about hobbies, told jokes, and laughed a lot. Sarah thought Yaron was both smart and funny. At the end of the evening, she told him, "You have beautiful eyes."

Key Phrases

- אפשר להזמין אותך לקפה? / Efshar Lehazmin Otach Lekafe? - Can I invite you for coffee?

- היה ממש כיף! / Haya Mamash Keif! - It was really fun!

- אולי ניפגש שוב? / Ulai Nipgash Shuv? - Maybe we can meet again?

Hobbies

Discussing hobbies is a fantastic way to break the ice, find common ground, and learn more about the people you meet.

Word Bank

- תחביב / Tachviv - Hobby

- מה התחביבים שלך? / Ma HaTachvivim Shelach? - What are your hobbies?

- לנגן / Lenagen - To play (an instrument)

- כינור / Kinor - Violin

- לתפור / Litpor - To sew

- לבשל / Levashel - To cook

- לאפות / Le'efot - To bake

- לשחק שחמט / Lesachek Schachmat - To play chess

- לטייל / Letayel - To travel/hike

- לצפות בסרטים / Litzpot BeSratim - To watch movies

Scenario 1:

- Person A: ?יש לך תחביבים מעניינים (Do you have any interesting hobbies?)

- Person B: אני אוהב/ת מאוד לבשל. אני מנסה מתכונים חדשים כל הזמן! (I love to cook. I try new recipes all the time!)

- Person A: גם אני! אולי נחליף מתכונים פעם? (Me too! Maybe we can exchange recipes sometime?)

Scenario 2:

- Person A: אני רוצה למצוא תחביב חדש. יש לך רעיונות? (I want to find a new hobby. Do you have any ideas?)

- Person B: מה לגבי צילום? או אולי כדai לך לנסות שיעורי יוגה? (How about photography? Or maybe you should try yoga classes?)

Key Phrases

- ...אני נהנה/נהנית מ / Ani Nehene/Nehenet Mi... - I enjoy...

- ...אני מתעניין/מתעניינת ב / Ani Mit'anyen/Mit'anyenet Be... - I'm interested in...

- ...תמיד רציתי לנסות / Tamid Ratziti Lenassot... - I've always wanted to try...

Chapter Summary

In this chapter, we took your Hebrew to the next level! We covered:

- Advanced possession and Biblical Hebrew.
- We also covered some basic vocabulary about blind dates and talking about hobbies - earning essential vocabulary and phrases to navigate blind dates and small-talk with ease.

Practice

Exercise 1:

Test your knowledge of the concepts we learned. For each question, choose the correct answer and provide the reason for your choice.

1. Translate the phrase "her voice" into Hebrew:

    ○ קול שלך

    ○ קולה

    ○ קולך

2. What does the phrase "ויאמר האיש" mean in English?

    ○ And the man loved
    ○ And the man said
    ○ And the man saw

3. Which possessive suffix would you add to the word "ספר" (book) to say "their book"?

    ○ -ם

    ○ -ךָ

    ○ -נו

4. Translate the phrase "his children" into Hebrew:

    ○ ילדים שלו

    ○ ילדיו

    ○ ילדותו

5. How would you say "my teacher" (female) in Hebrew?

- ○ מורתי
- ○ מורו
- ○ מורה שלי

Exercise 2:

Here's a story about blind dates with blanks for vocabulary/grammar practice, followed by comprehension questions:

דנה התכוננה לדייט העיוור שלה. היא לבשה את השמלה היפה _____ והתאפרה. היא הייתה קצת _____, אבל החליטה _____ את עצמה ואמרה: "יהיה בסדר!" כשהגיעה למסעדה, היא _____ בחור חמוד בשם איתי. הם _____ והתחילו לדבר. איתי סיפר שהוא עובד _____, ודנה סיפרה שהיא _____. אחרי שהם , איתי שילם את _____ והם יצאו מהמסעדה. "היה ממש כיף!" אמרה דנה. " להיפגש שוב?"

Word Bank

- שלה (her)
- ליהנות (to enjoy)
- התיישבו (sat down - plural)
- נרגשת (nervous)
- אולי (maybe)
- מהנדס (engineer)
- רופאה (doctor - female)
- אכלו (ate)

- ניפגש (we will meet)

- החשבון (the bill/check)

- ראה (saw)

Questions

1. איך הרגישה דנה לפני הדייט?

2. איפה נפגשו דנה ואיתי?

3. מה המקצוע של איתי?

4. מה המקצוע של דנה?

5. תאר/י מה עשו איתי ודנה במסעדה.

6. מי שילם בסוף הדייט?

7. האם לדעתך דנה ואיתי יהיו זוג? למה כן/למה לא?

Exercise 3:

Hobby Adventures

מיכל מאוד אהבה את הזמן הפנוי שלה. אחרי יום ארוך בעבודה, היא תמיד _____ משהו כיפי לעשות. היא _____ לצייר בסטודיו הקטן שלה. לפעמים היא _____ עם חברים לבית קפה, והם _____ על החיים. בימי שבת, מיכל אהבה לצאת _____ ארוכות בפארק. היא _____ את השקט של הטבע. מיכל גם _____ ספרים, במיוחד ספרי מתח. הערב, היא החליטה להישאר בבית ו_____ את הפרק הבא בסדרה האהובה עליה.

Word Bank

- לעשות (to do)

- הלכה (went - female)

- אוהבת (loves)

- לטייל (to hike/travel)

- צפתה (watched)

- קראה (read - female)

- מציירת (draws/paints - female)

- דיברו (talked)

Questions

1. מה מיכל עושה בזמנה הפנוי?

2. לאן היא אוהבת ללכת עם חברים?

3. מה מיכל עושה בימי שבת?

4. מה היא אוהבת לעשות כשהיא לבד?

5. סוג הספרים האהוב על מיכל הוא...

6. מה מיכל החליטה לעשות הערב?

7. איזה תחביב לא הוזכר בסיפור? תן/י דוגמה לתחביב נוסף שמיכל יכולה לאהוב.

Chapter 6 Answer Key

Exercise 1:

1. קולה (Reason: The correct possessive suffix for "her" is ה-)

2. **And the man said** (Reason: "ויאמר" means "and he said")

3. ם- (Reason: The suffix for "their" (masculine) is ם-)

4. ילדיו (Reason: The correct possessive suffix for "his" is ו-)

5. מורתי (Reason: The correct possessive suffix for "my" (feminine object) is י-)

Exercise 2:

Potential Story Answers

- שלה
- נרגשת
- ליהנות
- ראה
- התיישבו
- מהנדס
- רופאה
- אכלו
- החשבון
- אולי
- ניפגש

Question Answers

1. דנה הייתה נרגשת.

2. במסעדה.

3. איתי הוא מהנדס.

4. דנה היא רופאה.

5. הם ישבו, דיברו, ואכלו.

6. איתי שילם.

7. Answers will vary based on the reader's interpretation.

Exercise 3:

Potential Story Answers

- לעשות
- אוהבת
- מציירת
- הלכה
- דיברו
- לטייל
- צפתה
- קראה

Question Answers

1. מציירת, הולכת לבית קפה עם חברים, מטיילת, קוראת, צופה בטלוויזיה.

2. לבית קפה.

3. היא יוצאת לטיולים ארוכים בפארק.

4. לקרוא וצפות בטלוויזיה.

5. ספרי מתח.

6. לצפות בסדרה האהובה עליה.

7. לנגן, לשיר, לרקוד, לבשל, וכו'. Answers will vary. Examples:

Conclusion

The best way to learn a language is to use it.

הַדֶּרֶךְ הַטּוֹבָה בְּיוֹתֵר לִלְמֹד שָׂפָה הִיא לְהִשְׁתַּמֵּשׁ בָּהּ

Throughout this book, you've conquered the complexities of past and future tenses, explored the vibrant world of Israeli slang, and immersed yourself in the everyday Hebrew used on the streets of Israel. You're no longer just a Hebrew student; you're starting to think and express yourself like an Israeli.

Remember, language learning is a journey.

It certainly has been for me.

The more you speak, read, and listen to Hebrew, the more natural it will become. Don't be afraid to experiment, make mistakes, and most importantly, have fun with it!

Here are some ways to keep the momentum going:

- **Find a Language Partner:** Seek out native Hebrew speakers online or in your community for conversation practice.
- **Immerse Yourself in Israeli Media:** Watch Israeli movies and TV shows, listen to Israeli music, and read Hebrew news and literature.
- **Plan a Trip to Israel:** Experience the language in its natural environment and put your skills to the test. It will be 100% worth it, trust me!

The world of Hebrew is now open to you. From ordering a *shakshuka* at a bustling Tel Aviv Cafe to debating Israeli politics with new friends, your fluency will unlock countless experiences. The richer your understanding of Hebrew becomes, the deeper your connection to Israel and its people will grow.

Thank you for embarking on this 30-day Hebrew adventure! Let your passion for the language continue to flourish and may Hebrew open new doors of understanding and connection for you.

Made in the USA
Las Vegas, NV
02 November 2024

11004207R00171